SCHOODIC POINT

SCHOODIC POINT

HISTORY ON THE EDGE *of* ACADIA NATIONAL PARK

ALLEN K. WORKMAN

THE
History
PRESS

Published by The History Press
Charleston, SC 29403
www.historypress.net

Copyright © Allen K. Workman
All rights reserved

All images courtesy of the author unless otherwise noted.

Front cover, bottom: Courtesy of Flickr user alans1948.
Back cover, bottom: Courtesy of L. Peterson Photography.

First published 2014

ISBN 978.1.5402.1045.6

Library of Congress CIP data applied for.

CONTENTS

PREFACE

The story of the Schoodic Point region, which has been told only in small sections, has long needed a narrative that gives a full trajectory of the changes that have taken place here over the last four centuries. This history, an effort in that direction, grew first from the realization that the timeless beauty of the Schoodic we love is vulnerable to disruption and even destruction by the ongoing forces of change in human ecology. With this comes the belief that to fully appreciate and protect what we have, we must understand what has happened over time and, if possible, why.

This work emerged from the convergence of my private good fortune in helping map the region with my friend Tom Mayer and the public misfortune of a threatened resort development that would have choked off the park and disrupted the ecology of the Schoodic Point region. The latter was thankfully avoided (see Chapter 13), and the former gave this book some of Tom's fine cartography. As events unfolded and I gave some talks about Schoodic, I published part of the Point story in the Maine Historical Society's journal, *Maine History* (45:2, 96–122), spurred by my late friend Professor Emeritus Bob Babcock and thanks to Professor Richard Judd of the University of Maine History Department. In time, I was urged to fill out the story as a book by Schoodic Education and Research Center (SERC) staffers Bill Zoellick and especially Dr. Mike Soukup, who has steadily sponsored this project. The project has had continuous encouragement, support and reading from Acadia National Park staffers, especially cultural resources manager Rebecca Cole-Will, as well as from park botanists Jill

Weber, Glen Mittelhauser and Kate Miller. After some delay, the project now sees publication due to the perspicacity of my editors at The History Press, Katie Orlando and Will Collicott, but also with inspiration from my naturalist daughter Amy's artwork and because of clear-eyed reading from my most insightful and loving editor, Jean.

A.K.W.
February 14, 2014

OUT AT THE END:
A PREAMBLE

E ast of Bar Harbor, across the bay from the mountainous island that Champlain in 1604 named "Mount Desert," a high promontory reaches far out to sea, rising dramatically over four hundred feet to dominate the horizon. Though Champlain did not name this bold eastern promontory, he accurately mapped his discovery to show how this far-out point and adjacent islands formed a fearsome barrier of ocean currents and heavy surf threatening coastal navigators. "Cape Furious" (Cape Enrage) was a name

A view of Schoodic Point on the horizon from the east.

reportedly given this point by later French chart-makers. Of course, native people had navigated this ocean barrier long before Champlain. Among the most aggressive of these were the Mi'kmaq warriors who, on their many raids southwestward, may have named this promontory *Eskwodek*—"the end" or "point of land"—a name that subsequent French and English navigators transformed on charts to approximate our modern name for the Point and its nearby region: Schoodic.[1]

THE SCHOODIC POINT REGION

Today, this name properly designates the remote outer Schoodic Point itself, as well as the broader Point region, an isolated and barely inhabited area that lies between the nearby settlements of Birch Harbor and Winter Harbor, south of Route 186. The region is dominated by 430-foot Schoodic Head Mountain and the surrounding hills around the ridge of Birch Harbor Mountain immediately to its north, forming a green band of forest and shore that defines the peninsular Schoodic Point region.

SCHOODIC: A LANDSCAPE BEYOND TIME?

For many, the Point region has seemed a faraway and timeless landscape of natural splendor, a place of elemental beauty apparently untouched by the uncertainties of changing events. Some also have regarded Schoodic as a scientific laboratory of nature, a place for empirical observation of its basic processes and cycles. For almost everyone, the Point region has been firmly associated with the beauty of a preserve at its center, the eastern section of Acadia National Park. Yet the land has been in this preserved state for well short of a century, and much of it was ready for preservation only by the first decade of the twenty-first century. In fact, the land at Schoodic looks back over a long period of changes in the last four hundred years—slowly in the first two centuries but quite rapidly in the last two—and almost entirely due to human intervention. The region witnessed steady development and settlement as a busy part of the local and regional economy before it became preserved, somewhat by accident, and integrated into Acadia National Park.

Signs of Change at Schoodic

Our easy access from busy resorts into the remote, unspoiled scenery at Schoodic should suggest to a thoughtful person that such beauty must have come to us only through some interesting transformations. And a very curious visitor might soon notice signs that things were once different: features in the Point's landscape that are now nearly invisible, revealed only by the old cellar holes, remnants of abandoned roadways and fields and partially cleared or newly forested areas. These remains, as well as some obscure documents, reveal that Acadia National Park at Schoodic is the scene of a once lively village cluster that was slowly overtaken and absorbed into the Park and surrounding timberland. In fact, one of the more extensive ghost town village environments found along Maine's public shoreland is now incorporated into Acadia National Park here.[2]

Discovering How the Point Has Changed

Today, a diligent visitor could eventually find evidence that, however primitive this conserved land of forested shoreline may still appear, it has over time endured many severe impacts of civilization on its environment: timber cutting, farming, a fish processing plant, harbor facilities, extensive human settlement and substantial prospects for development into recreational resort real estate. Past records show that today's quiet, largely uninhabited parkland has thus far outlasted the grand designs of three enormously wealthy capitalists. And it has witnessed the efforts of generations of Americans who inhabited and worked on this land, most of them striving to cope with the pressures of a worldwide commercial marketplace. Considering so much development, it might seem astonishing that anything survives today of Schoodic's most vulnerable asset—the primal, nearly untouched appearance of its landscape as we see it.

THE REWARDS OF LOOKING AT SCHOODIC'S PAST

Schoodic offers a distinctive combination—natural beauty seemingly beyond civilization, which has nevertheless survived nearly invisible layers of human occupation. Now, a little poking into the many remnants of Schoodic's past will allow us to recover a coherent narrative of its survival. Our awareness of the Point's spectacular surroundings will gain depth by seeing it through the added dimension of time. Examining Schoodic's changes is the best way to develop a full appreciation for what we have and for what it will take to handle the relentless cycles of pressure for development and preservation that has affected how we experience the Schoodic environment today. In this process, it is important to gain a sense of the fragility of this preserved land, whose seemingly timeless beauties cannot be taken for granted. By observing what has happened to Schoodic's human ecology over time, we can discover some recurrent patterns in how the land has lived through its evolving cycles and thus gain a sense of confidence in our ability to handle and anticipate the changes that will come.

CHAPTER 1

DISCOVERING THE SCHOODIC LANDSCAPE

For most visitors, a trip to Schoodic is a small voyage of discovery, even for those who come repeatedly to gain a new experience in its shifting atmospheric conditions or in finding a detail previously unseen. But all who come to Schoodic find that a key to the character of the outer Point's landscape is its remoteness as a land reaching far out to sea. Called "Schoodic Peninsula" by early owners, the Point region has the appropriate characteristic of that term, of being "almost an island." Today's visitors can easily believe they are surrounded by ocean as they stand looking seaward from the tip of the Point. This far-out spot in earlier times was almost unreachable from the mainland by foot, blocked as it is by a shoreline of high cliffs and thick mountainous forests that still surround the outer end. Even as we reach it with relative ease today, Schoodic continues as a world of its own, preserved by its remoteness and isolation from surrounding coastal towns and resorts.

From the earliest times, people's views of Schoodic have been closely related to its physical features, its possibilities for passage and habitation as well as its economically exploitable resources. Native canoeists and European mariners may well have been awed by the striking shoreline and landscape at Schoodic. Yet at the same time, they had to deal realistically with the Point's perils as the formidable edge of a passage to elsewhere and with its limitations as a relatively unpromising and unfruitful shore in a marginal terrain. The land that greeted them at Schoodic, typical of most of the region's islands and promontories, had lost much of its soil and had

Schoodic Point as seen across Schoodic Harbor from Wonsqueak.

tirent de l'ifle S. Croix le dernier iour d'Aouſt
audict an 1604.

DE LA COSTE, PEVPLES ET RIVIERE DE NO-
rembeque: & de tout ce qui c'eſt paſſé durant les deſcouuertures d'icelle.

C H A P. V.

APres le partement des vaiſſeaux, le ſieur
de Mons ſe delibera d'enuoyer deſcouurir
le long de la coſte de Norembegue, pour ne
perdre temps : & me commit ceſte charge,
que i'eus fort aggreable.

deſquelles ſont couuertes de pins & ſapins, &
autres meſchants bois. Parmy ces iſles y a force
beaux & bós ports, mais mal-aggreables pour
y demeurer. Ce meſme iour nous paſſames
auſſi proche d'vne iſle qui contient enuiron 4.
ou cinq lieux de lóg, auprés laquelle nous nous
cuidames perdre ſur vn petit rocher à fleur
d'eau, qui fit vne ouuerture à noſtre barque
proche de la quille. De ceſte iſle iuſques au
nord de la terre ferme il n'y a pas cét pas de large. Elle eſt fort haute couppee par endroicts,

In the framed section are Champlain's views on Schoodic's terrain. He noted that the area had nice harbors but that the timber was poor and it would be hard to live there. *From* Les Voyages du Sieur de Champlain *(1613)*.

its south-facing rock stripped off by ancient south-moving glaciers, leaving dramatic heights of granite confronting the sea. Unlike the glacial deposits of soil and gravel at Mount Desert and its outer islands, what remains of the Point's geology is a relatively thin and barren covering of needles and crumbly granitic gravel, professionally called "Schoodic soil." Inland from the shore, boggy depressions in the bedrock give enough moisture, thin soil and sustenance for uneven forests. These are mainly of spruce, fir and tamarack, as well as jack pine (at its southernmost reach), birch, cedar, a few maple and very little surviving white pine. While this is enough to support a little wildlife at the edge of the sea, it has been discouraging to human settlement.[3]

Champlain's 1604 impression of the archipelago of islands and peninsulas just east of Mount Desert gives a clear view of what potential for economic development Europeans would find at Schoodic. Comparing the region unfavorably with the oaks and hardwoods of more desirable terrain, the explorer described the far-reaching stretches of isles and peninsulas including Schoodic as "mostly covered with pines, firs, spruces and other woods of inferior quality." He thought the area offered "very fine and worthy harbors, but poorly suited as a place to live." His words seem to make a neat summary of the exploitable natural resources available to later nineteenth-century settlers of an outer peninsula like Schoodic: an isolated, marginal place far out to sea with some mediocre timber, usable fishing harbors and a soil on which it would be hard to live. This was to be the combination that contributed both to Schoodic's preservation and to the development of its barely sustainable economic resources until the late 1800s.[4]

By the nineteenth century, developers and settlers were indeed endeavoring to live on Schoodic's thin resources, testing its economic limits and trying to reach a sort of balance with the land and available maritime resources. In time, the settlers all but gave up on the meager development possibilities of the Point environment and by the late 1880s were slowly moving away. But another level of experiencing the landscape was about to play a new role. Prosperous city people, becoming aware of the disappearance of undeveloped or wild land, turned toward the natural world for recreation as an escape from an intensely developed urban and suburban scene. Relatively undisturbed coastal Maine land for vacationing resorts became a commercial commodity, but along with this development came a genuine appreciation for experiencing the unique, the exotic, the remote and the uncluttered feeling of a natural landscape. In the 1890s, a journalist accustomed to celebrating the arrival of big new resorts on open land near Bar Harbor was nevertheless able to express this rising level of awareness for the undeveloped beauties of Schoodic:

> *To the eastward one sees...beautiful islands. Then comes a grand sweep of ocean, and then...at one's feet lie the beautiful island studded waters of Frenchman's Bay, with the hills of Mount Desert in the background. Eleven lighthouses can be seen from the summit on a clear day...The extreme southern end of the peninsula is worth visiting even in moderate weather. Nowhere can one get a better idea of the tremendous force of the waves than here on this great stretch of bare ledge sloping inland, for over two hundred feet, to an elevation of thirty feet...bordered at the top by a wall of rocks thrown up by the waves. Some of these rocks weigh many hundred pounds.*

Out of this sensibility another level of land appreciation was becoming more explicit, encouraging people to treasure the spectacular Schoodic environment and let it survive for its own sake, eventually preserving it even for the benefit of the general public. But Schoodic Point, long preserved by its remoteness, had to pass through the rise and fall of many phases of economic development before it was ready for preservation.[5]

Frazer Cove, site of Schoodic's Lower Harbor village, a future dried-fish processing plant and many dwellings.

Indeed, the remote Schoodic Point region went through its own accelerated version of what happened to most New England open land: European discovery, exploitation and logging, extensive occupation and development by settlers and, later, economic abandonment for better lands elsewhere. But most of the Schoodic Point region has not followed the drift of much abandoned New England land, back into the commercial market to become gentrified or suburbanized. Instead it has come through many transformations to live on as a preserved natural environment, due to a distinctive combination of events. Over the course of three centuries, the land was touched by the heavy hand of three entrepreneurial tycoons—William Bingham, John G. Moore and John D. Rockefeller Jr.—each imposing his own kind of order on rough conditions. They, as well as two generations of Yankee settlers, created the conditions for a preserved landscape at Schoodic—a setting capable of allowing its visitors to feel that time here might stand still.

Furthermore: A Cycle of Development and Preservation at Schoodic

As with much open land in Maine, people over time have experienced Schoodic Point on two levels. Now and in the past, this land has been looked at both for its direct and concrete economic value and also for its natural beauty as a place to visit or stay to appreciate its undisturbed ecological integrity. Given the marginal terrain that Champlain saw on Schoodic Point and other peninsulas to the east, it might seem uncertain whether anyone would ever see such land as worth developing for economic gain. It would seem more likely to languish as a relatively undeveloped wasteland until its recreational or ecological value might be recognized in more recent times. As it happened, however, the Schoodic Point region has passed through a cycle of several such phases, both of extensive economic development and various degrees of disuse and passive preservation of its environment.

Commonly, an attractive but long-deserted terrain that has long been seen as unable to provide any immediate productive value is acquired by preservationists at relatively little cost as recreational ground, before its appeal becomes spoiled by wanton or wasteful uses in a kind of "tragedy of the commons." This was the pattern for our first national park at Yellowstone and also in Maine for such near-uninhabited areas as the duneland of Popham Beach or perhaps much of the cliff-lined shore of the Cutler Coast.

But almost equally often, such appealing but deserted land has undergone a series of stages. First, even marginal land like that at Schoodic is likely to see its thin resources extracted for economic gain and integrated into a network of economic productivity. Then at some point, the productivity of such land may languish, and its economic value may suffer a hiatus before undergoing a transformation, perhaps becoming commercially valuable again as a resort for recreation. At that point, to take the land out of the short-term economic mainstream and conserve its longer-term benefits for a broader constituency, people with a preservation motive must organize resources to avoid its further development, as happened in various ways at Acadia National Park. And eventually, to survive some of its maintenance costs and gain a public constituency, such land may need to develop a well-balanced niche in the tourist or modern preservationist economy. Even so, preserved land may continually risk being "loved to death" and engulfed by a surrounding economy of development, a continuing risk for many of our national parks.

Such a cyclic process, which may be typical for much preserved open land in Maine, fits the story of the land at Schoodic Point. But Schoodic, one of the earliest conserved with private funds for recreation, arrived at its development and preservation in its own distinctive way.

CHAPTER 2

CHANGES IN THE LAND
AT SCHOODIC

Today, thanks mainly to Acadia National Park, much of Schoodic's natural landscape may, in part, resemble what its early visitors saw in 1600. Then as now to an eagle's view, a forested land drops off, abruptly eastward and more broadly westward, from the summit of Schoodic Head Mountain, Birch Harbor Mountain's ridges and the sea-facing Anvil bluffs—heights that can make a weather barrier on either side, depending on fog and wind conditions. On both east and west sides of Schoodic Head, shallow salt ponds and mudflats (East Pond and West Pond) are sheltered by small islands (Little Moose and Pond Islands). A brackish marsh, connecting these ponds, lies behind the outer headland (Big Moose "Island"), whose seaward ledges are white-rimmed from the spectacular crashing surf of the open Atlantic.

The view north of Schoodic Head shows the extensive hilly forestland and wetland around Birch Harbor Mountain and Pond, the Point's ecological green belt link to the mainland on the north. This section has come to be called the "Schoodic Woods." Just offshore to the southeast stretches Schoodic Island, the outermost barrier to navigation, while to the northeast, a small island and an adjoining point (Wonsqueak or Spruce Point) shape a bay and the two small harbors (Wonsqueak and Bunkers) to the east. Across the water, to the northwest beyond Schoodic, a cluster of islands (Turtle, Mark and Heron) and a sizable headland (Grindstone Neck) form the bay now called Winter Harbor, and farther westward across Frenchman Bay on the horizon are the high mountains of Mount Desert. The shores of the Schoodic Point region as they run northward on both sides alternate

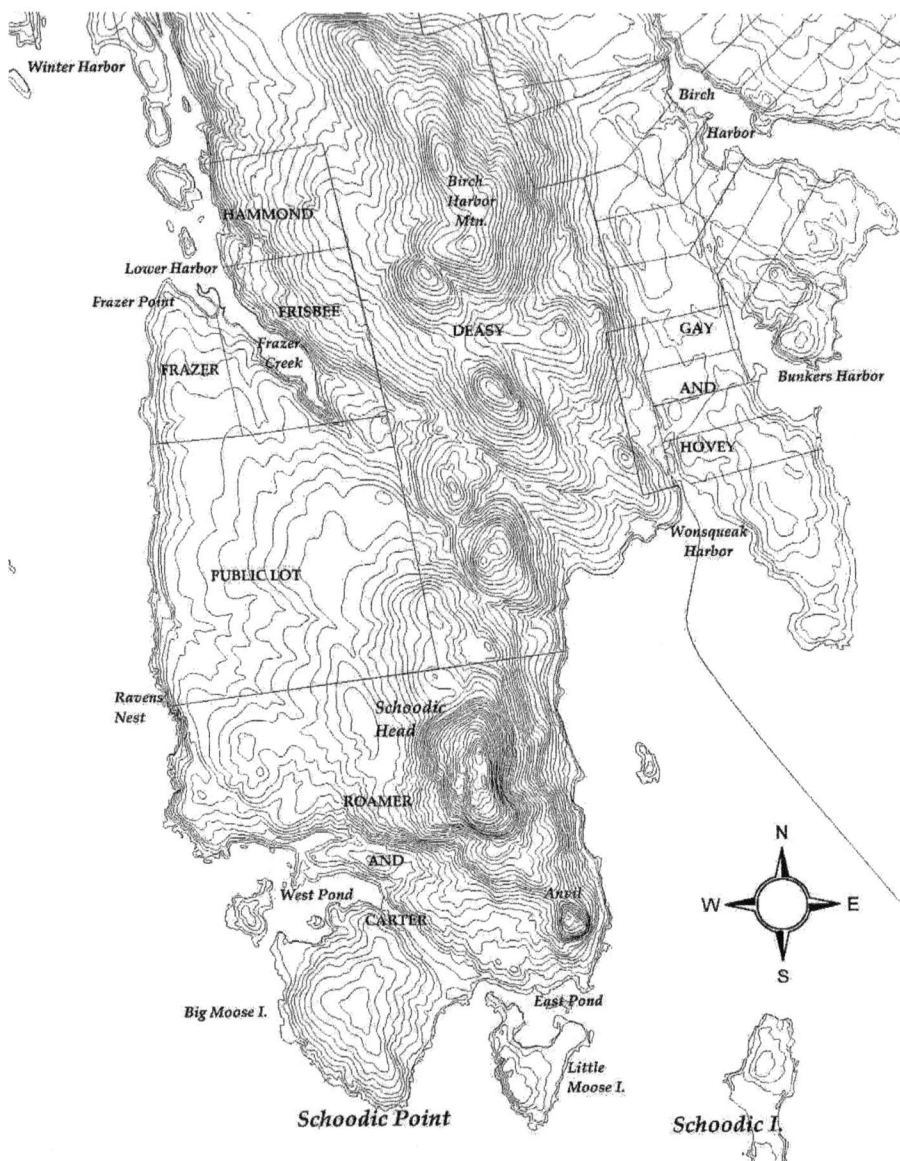

A map of the Schoodic Point region showing names and properties of the original purchasers as surveyed by Isaac Coolidge in 1798. *Map by Thomas Mayer.*

between high-rising stone bluffs or slopes and rough stone beaches, isolating the tip of the peninsula. About a mile northward on the Point's west side, the shore is broken by a small harbor and creek, eventually called Frazer Cove and Frazer Creek for its first settler.

The unique, almost sub-arctic boreal ecology of the outer Point and islands is critically shaped by its relation to the broader Schoodic Point region that surrounds it. A green band of uninhabited hilly forestland lies two to four miles thick to the north of Schoodic Head Mountain, insulating the outer Point from the nearest villages of Wonsqueak, Bunkers and Winter Harbors. This uninhabited band of forestland, the Schoodic Woods clustered around the long ridge of Birch Harbor Mountain and its watershed, distinctively isolates the outer peninsula of Schoodic Point from the rest of the mainland. At the same time, though it has been heavily logged, this forestland conducts a steady flow of plant and animal life toward the outer Point, sustaining the entire area in a critical ecologically balanced tension. The peninsular character of the Point region creates environmental conditions that gradually become harsher along the shore and toward the tip, with mainland vegetation thinning until the outer reaches resemble the fragility and sparseness found on remote islands. The spare outer tip is thus in delicate balance with the interior, allowing a limited passage for visiting moose, bear, deer and smaller mammals, while enabling distinctive plant species such as jack pine to reach its southern coastal limit at Schoodic. Meanwhile, the surrounding ocean gives the Schoodic Point region much of the nourishment for its wildlife: small mammals and birds scavenging the shoreline in close connection with diverse marine animals and fish.[6]

FOUR CENTURIES OF CHANGE IN THE SCHOODIC LANDSCAPE

Even if much of the Schoodic Point region may appear to have reverted to something like a primordial state, some of its ecology has undergone substantial change along with steady warming since the "Little Ice Age" climate of 1600. Schoodic's red granite mountains, outcroppings and coastline provide a strong resistance to erosion, with many distinctive intrusions of softer, fine-grained iron and magnesium-rich basalt dikes. But to the northwest, some portions of the shore are of softer gravel that

A heavily sea-eroded bank in Frazer Cove on which lobster-pound buildings stood only a generation ago.

rising seas have crumbled away, silting in what had been a deeper harbor, especially at Frazer Cove. Meanwhile, much of its animal and plant life has seen some significant changes over four centuries. The evidence for this, especially for larger animals, has been revealed by archaeological findings in the region, as well as in records left by early explorers and later by hunters and naturalists. Such sources—some specific to Schoodic and others more broadly regional—suggest that many of the changes in nature at the Point have been due to human causes.

Animal Populations

Evidently, much of the visible fauna at Schoodic has varied little from what was reported in earlier times—bears, rabbits, porcupines, raccoons and a majority of our seabirds have persisted in the region, though some population changes are harder to determine over a long period. But populations for some of the largest mammals that frequented Schoodic have undergone very great transformations since the 1600s, most notably the ungulates—deer, moose and caribou. Trading post reports for Machias, some forty miles to the east, show that from the 1770s through the 1790s, there were twenty times more moose hides taken than deer, along with some caribou pelts. This shows that deer were relatively scarce at Schoodic, composing only 5 percent of the ungulate population until moose were nearly hunted out of the region in the 1860s before being protected by game laws. By then, deer had filled the vacancy, in large part because deer forage had become more common and accessible due to heavy timber cutting of denser evergreen forests. But deer also had a special role in dispatching the local population of caribou. A few of these broad-footed lichen eaters survived in the Ellsworth area until the 1890s, while they were reported as "common" near Machias until the 1840s. But some ten years later, the previously scarce deer population had completely displaced caribou, probably by bringing in the devastating brainworm parasite, which does not harm deer but is carried through their feces, frequently ingested by the close-cropping ground feeding of moose and caribou. The result has been a total disappearance of caribou throughout Maine, while moose continue to suffer a toll from the brainworm parasite.[7]

The predators that fed on deer around Schoodic have also changed dramatically since 1600, when a few wolverine hides were traded at Machias. Wolves were also reported in the area, though they were effectively gone by the mid-nineteenth century. The last timber wolf was reported in the Union River area in 1870, to be replaced by an increasing population of coyotes. The eastern cougar, now declared extinct, would not have been in the Schoodic vicinity after the eighteenth century, despite some breathless anecdotal sightings. Any such reports might have involved visits from incoming western cougars but more likely were viewings of the still scarce lynx, reported as "common" in the Mount Desert area in the 1850s and still bounty-hunted into the 1920s. In fact, these animals, often mistaken for the much more common bobcat, are now scarce even in Northern Maine and subsist largely on snowshoe rabbits. As a potential deer hunter, the lynx in the North country had been given the Francophone name loup-cervier (deer-wolf), Anglicized to "lucifee" and eventually "devil-cat" or "Indian-devil," under which names it was hunted as a sheep predator at Schoodic Point in the 1880s.

Other larger fauna from early days were driven out, decimated or hunted to extinction, most notably the great auk and passenger pigeon. But the large otter-sized sea mink, prized for its pelt by settlers, has also suffered extinction. At Schoodic, its bones were found in a pre-contact Native American midden, along with the bones of now scarce right whale, sturgeon, cod and haddock. Other animals seen nearby in Maine by early explorers, yet driven out while surviving elsewhere, include the whistling swan and whooping crane. Prominent returnees to Schoodic today include the moose, river otter, a few fisher and the beaver, whose pelts were a plentifully traded commodity at Machias in the 1790s and beyond. Consequently, beavers disappeared here until reestablished in the twentieth century, especially in the marshes at Wonsqueak Harbor and creeks flowing into West Pond.[8]

Sea bird populations have varied considerably, including our common herring gull, whose numbers were much reduced in the nineteenth century by the fashion for pure white feather clusters for ladies hats. Now protected, gulls were extensively taken for their feather breasts and sold by Passamaquoddy and Penobscot hunters in market tents at Bar Harbor until the 1920s. Eider duck populations, scarce in the early 1900s, resurgent in the 1960s and now thinner, have fluctuated widely and will continue to be studied by researchers at Schoodic along with other migrating and resident birds. However, one of the most common animal populations at the Point from the 1840s to the early 1900s has now completely disappeared: those herded on early farms and pastures. Cattle and especially sheep were once abundant herds at Schoodic until farms were gradually abandoned in the region.[9]

Changes in Forest and Field

The forest of the early 2000s that persists in the Point region has a distinctive range of abundant large tree species. Most dominant are spruces of three varieties that, in geological terms, became prolific in eastern Maine relatively recently, replacing hemlocks as the most dominant species between one thousand and five hundred years ago, just a few centuries before European settlement. At Schoodic, however, spruces became established several millennia earlier than elsewhere downeast; pollen analysis at the Point has found spruces to be a well-established species here as long as five to six thousand years ago, several millennia before becoming so on Mount Desert Island. Some two or three thousand years back, a change in moisture balance allowed spruces to completely displace hemlocks, now a missing species in the Point region. It would appear that for several thousand years,

The hardy jack pine (*Pinus banksiana*), a pitch pine able to survive in drought, poor soil and granite environments. Schoodic is the southernmost terrain where the jack pine grows in profusion.

the far-out terrain at Schoodic has had a fog-bound climate that is distinct from elsewhere in the Acadia region.[10]

The forest at Schoodic is clearly no longer "primeval" or old growth and, in fact, has been extensively cut over. Like many other coastal forests in remote islands of the Acadia region, its timber resources have been logged both for clearing settlement land and marketing both lumber and especially firewood to stoke the limekilns of Rockland. Where a forest on an outlying Acadian shore has grown back on preserved land, it is still possible to trace early consumption of the woodland using precise GPS mapping and tree boring, as has been done recently for Long Island in Blue Hill Bay. For Schoodic, however, the use of early maps and land development records shows the pattern of logging quite clearly.[11]

The earliest substantial clear-cutting in the Point region occurred first at Frazer Cove before the 1830s. Soon afterward, there was major clearing at outer Schoodic Point around West and East Ponds and at the two Moose

Islands, as well as in the section around Bunkers and Wonsqueak Harbors. In many stretches along the road south of Frazer Cove, thick-growing tiny trunks reveal recent growth on former pasture and meadowlands. Elsewhere near West Pond, former farmland and meadows are grown up in alders, and Big Moose Island has seen a succession of clearing since its original farm became a U.S. Navy base and, more recently, a park center. On the other hand, the steep slopes and ledges on the east side of the outer Point, with a bluff shore difficult to reach from a few stone beaches, experienced relatively light logging. This unpromising ground is much grown up with Schoodic's distinctive drought-tolerant pitch pine species, the jack pine.

The most consistently logged area has been along the slopes of Birch Harbor Mountain, the Schoodic Woods land north of Schoodic Head, with generally fewer and younger trees and only an occasional tree as old as 120 years. Here, three recent logging efforts are recorded just since the 1960s. In the same area, small fires took a toll around 1930, but little or no evidence has been found for major burning in the Point area in recent times.

While the spruces still dominate the Point region's forest, also abundant are balsam fir, jack pine on ledge and thin soil and white cedar or red maple on moist slopes or bogs. Especially prolific are birches of all varieties, as well as larch or tamarack, balsam poplar and aspen. Other hardwoods are essentially missing, as are hemlocks, and while very few white pines can be found, there are even fewer red pines, mainly colonizing along logging roadways on the western slopes of the Birch Mountain forestland and at Bunkers Harbor. The answer to the question of whether these scanty species existed previously or were completely logged out as commercially valuable might be determined by further series of pollen studies. The jack pine (*Pinus banksiana*), by far the most distinctive tree at Schoodic, is found here at essentially its southern limit on the Atlantic coast, where it has been studied since the 1890s. It occupies the ecological niche that elsewhere is filled by pitch pine, able to tolerate arid conditions due to a thick needle or leaf that retains moisture in cold, rocky, dry terrain. Jack pines can grow straight and moderately tall but often take on picturesque, Bonsai-like bent shapes on ledges and bluffs. Such contorted growth has mostly spared them from logging, but their bark is often attacked by porcupines as a favored winter food. The notoriety of this tree's association with the Point region has now been established by nurserymen, who have developed a dwarf cultivar of the species known as "Schoodic" on the unlikely assumption that this stunted garden variety could be found wild in the Point region.

In Schoodic's marginal growing terrain, *Rosa rugosa* grows in a granite crevice with a stone flower sedum and the increasingly rare *Iris hookeri*.

A large variety of lower-growing trees or shrubs are common in the Schoodic Point region: mountain ash, alder, viburnum, eastern shad, mountain holly, winterberry and others. Open areas are commonly covered with huckleberry, bayberry, meadowsweet and other heath plants. Smaller flowering plants, recently the subject of ongoing research at the park's SERC facility, have only been systematically studied at Schoodic since the 1960s and comprehensively recorded in 2010. However, this area does share many species with Acadia National Park on Mount Desert Island that have been examined since the 1880s and '90s. It has been estimated that any given area in or around the park might lose or reconfigure up to 20 percent of its species population over a century, and certainly more in disturbed places. In fact, the protection of the national park there has not influenced this pattern, for such plant populations have changed as frequently within the park as in unprotected lands outside.

One common pattern of change for plants in the park area and beyond has been the gradual crowding out of more native species by those more recently introduced. Plants that were "uncommon" there in the 1890s are very often now rare or extinct, while some formerly unknown species have become invasive. At Schoodic in the early twenty-first century, this pattern had not yet become widespread. A few introduced or invasive species were found in areas disturbed by construction during the 1930s, at Frazer Point and at the nearby truck road power path. These were being monitored by park-sponsored botanists in order to forestall any potential threat of invasive effects with ongoing changes in climate.[12]

FORCES FOR CHANGE IN THE SCHOODIC ECOSYSTEM

Clearly there have long been a number of influential forces for change in the ecology of the Schoodic Point region, and there will be no end to the effects of the many possible natural processes. These include such factors as climate and sea level change, storm damage, fire, altered patterns of pollination, soil and water acidity and animal incursions by beaver, deer, porcupines, raccoons and insects. All these are likely, with other shifts in ecological conditions, to affect vulnerable, scanty plant populations in such stressed peninsular landscapes as Schoodic's. These forces are part of what some call "a wild natural environment," but many of the most disruptive processes have been influenced directly or indirectly by humans. Major changes at Schoodic were initiated by people in specific areas—through farming in four locations, fish processing at Frazer Cove, logging everywhere (but intensively around Birch Harbor Mountain and the Schoodic Woods), as well as through numerous roadways and buildings, all involving some pollutants or the release of domestic plant and animal species. And by no means least of human influences are recreational visitor impacts since the 1890s. Because of these human factors, a full appreciation of what we are looking at in the Schoodic region's landscape requires knowing more about people's activity in key sectors of the Point region.

FURTHERMORE: SIGNS OF CIVILIZATION IN THE SCHOODIC WOODS

In the nearly uninhabited forest of the Schoodic Point region, one can find many clues to the kinds of human activities that occurred years ago. The most obvious are remnants of structures and castaway hardware, as well

An apple tree next to Thomas Arey's abandoned homestead at "Schoodic Farm" on today's Alder Trail.

as old roads or pathways, stone walls and sawn logs and stumps. A useful handbook for identifying such clues is *Reading the Forested Landscape*, by Tom Wessels, whose illustrated text provides rich detail about layers of forest growth and disturbance, as well as about signs of human activity in stone walls and fences. At Schoodic, there are few such man-made artifacts beyond the built-up areas by roads and buildings, but the growing forest itself can reveal much about earlier human activity.

While the signs of recent logging or clear-cutting are usually quite obvious, these fade over a generation as wood rots and growth resumes. In the Schoodic Point region, an area of spruces that was once extensively logged or damaged by storms is likely to show a thick patch of fast-growing slim birches or perhaps balsam firs. Plots of disturbed soil from former field, pasture or roadway are often grown up in alders and other shrubs. A large spruce surrounded by much smaller growth may suggest that the big tree has been left standing in the midst of an area that has been cleared for farming or pasture. In a logged-over conifer forest, the roots of spruce or balsam fir are killed, leaving few traces of the lumberjack when their remains rot or disintegrate over time. However, the roots of birch or maple hardwoods survive cutting, throwing out multiple shoots that often grow into trees of two or three trunks. These give evidence of an area that has survived earlier cutting, with the space between the base of multiple trunks a sign of the size of the original hardwood.

But by far the most reliable sign in the forest for the one-time presence of domestic activity is the humble apple tree. An apple does not originate as a wild plant and wherever found in the woods has almost certainly been planted by a settler nearby. Such a tree found in the forest may be quite old or even a seedling or regrown branch of a parent tree long dead, but it is a sure sign that someone wanted to pick apples in the area. There are several in the woods in or near the Acadia National Park district at Schoodic, as well as in areas still settled. Two or three are still in the forest by the former village of Lower Harbor near old foundations, another two along the shore near West Pond and again by the foundations at Schoodic Farm along today's Alder Path. There is even a struggling survivor along a path on the outer shore at Big Moose Island in the former Navy base, at the edge of an old pasture. Looking for apple tree remnants in the Point region is an intriguing way to discover ghosts of settlers past.

CHAPTER 3

SCHOODIC IN THE LAND
OF THE WABANAKI

B y the time the shoreland of the Schoodic Point region had rebounded
from the weight of glaciers and reached the sea level of the modern
era, the people arriving there may have seen a raw landscape of granite
and conifer distantly resembling our view of today. We can assume that the
ancestors of our Passamaquoddy and Penobscot people fully appreciated a
primeval beauty in the Point region, but they seem to have lived here only
intermittently and not in large group settlements as elsewhere along the
coast. Shell-heap middens found by Acadia National Park archaeologists
indicate small group habitation from an early period long before European
contact. Those in the Schoodic District of the park reveal the existence
of small seasonal dwelling sites as old as 3,000 years ago and as recent as
1,200 years ago. At Wonsqueak and near Winter Harbor, a few artifacts and
rhyolite workings have turned up along with minor shell heaps, suggesting
visits in more recent times from small groups or families for clamming,
fishing, hunting and berrying.[13]

Food production and navigation, basic activities for native people in the
region, are major themes that underlie two interpretations for the name of
the point that became "Schoodic" on English maps. Elsewhere in Maine,
the Wabanaki name *scoudiac* indicates a place associated with fire, and if
applied to the Point region as claimed by Penobscot historians, the term
would indicate a "burnt place" for hunting, berrying or perhaps even some
form of horticulture. But other linguists familiar with native place names
feel this term would be less applicable to the Point setting than the Mi'kmaq

"Shallop" vessels like this replica were owned and navigated by Mi'kmaqs, who sailed past Schoodic to raid and trade westward in the early 1600s. *Photo from ilxor.com.*

name *esquodek*, applied by these frequent sojourners to mean "the end" of land to be navigated. French allies of the Mi'kmaq evidently incorporated this term for the peninsula to show "Pointe Escoudet" on a map in 1704. Yet an English explorer of the 1620s supported the fire theme in an engraving showing native people near Bar Harbor setting fire to the woods to drive game. Though scientific surveys show no major scorching fires in the region since the twelfth century, small and rapid fires were well-documented native methods for driving deer and moose, clearing growth for berry picking or creating habitat to encourage game. Both terms, which may have been merged by English mapmakers, are well suited to basic concerns of native people at Schoodic—their need to modify the land for its possibilities as a hunting ground and to avoid its hazards as a navigational frontier.[14]

Certainly coastal navigation was a major preoccupation of native peoples both before European contact and afterward as northern and eastern tribes sought corn and other commodities from the south in exchange for hunting goods. Trade navigation around Schoodic Point intensified as Mi'kmaq groups to the northeast, controlling the supply of European trade goods, sought to monopolize coastal commerce in these scarce commodities. By 1600, they had mastered the use of heavy European shallop sloops, which were sailed by all-native crews past the Schoodic region, encountering English traders as far south as Cape Cod. Yet all the Wabanaki groups were expert canoe navigators and could skirt past Schoodic Point in the worst of weather using portages in the region. To avoid canoeing around turbulent waters at the outer points, travelers seem to have used traditional portages between West and East Ponds behind Big Moose Island and possibly between Wonsqueak and Bunkers Harbors. Such canoe navigation continued into the early 1900s as native family groups were reported as camping at Wonsqueak and the Point en route to trading westward at the tourist market at Bar Harbor.

By the time of Champlain's arrival past Schoodic in 1604, native trading in the Point region was no longer peaceful—Schoodic had turned into a hostile frontier. The Mi'kmaq, shifting from protecting their monopoly in French cookware, firearms and weapons, turned to raiding southwestern tribes for corn and other goods while forcing nearby eastern tribes, including the Passamaquoddy, into an aggressive collaboration known by their victims as "Tarrentine." In response, the Penobscots and southwestern Wabanaki formed the defensive Mawooshen confederacy, with a deserted Schoodic Point on their eastern front line. In this situation, the French explorer found no human habitation in this frontier Point region or for many miles to the east. His translator-guides from the Passamaquoddy area had to speak with cautious diplomacy to the closely related Penobscots whom Champlain met at Mount Desert Island. Twenty years later, the power of all the tribal groups had been severely weakened by European diseases, and the French and English colonizers had begun dominating trade in the area as they did for more than a century afterward.

Schoodic continued on the margin as a frontier region between the two rival European powers until the early eighteenth century. On the eve of the French and Indian Wars of the 1690s, the English governor from Boston came to the Cranberry Islands and Placentia to assert his sovereignty and to confront the leading French claimant to the area, Sieur de la Mothe Cadillac. The Islanders told him that Cadillac was living "on the eastern side" at a place called "Winskeag Bay." Antiquarians of the 1920s assumed this must indicate somewhere on Mount Desert Island (possibly Otter Creek Point),

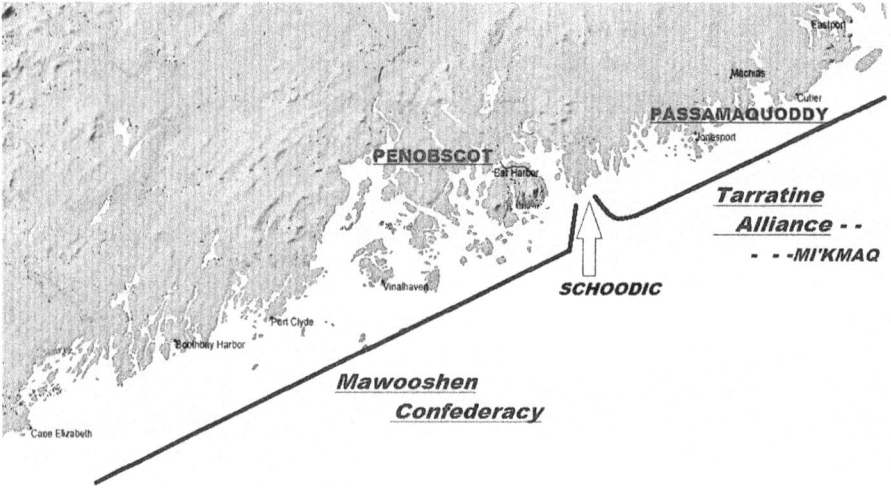

Schoodic shown in the early 1600s at the borderline of the war between the Mi'kmaqs and the Penobscots and their western allies—the Mawooshen Confederacy.

Sieur de la Mothe Cadillac at Schoodic and "Winskeag," as shown on a 1932 decorative map. *Extract of map by L.S. Phillips, courtesy of M.J. Smith.*

yet no place on the island today has a name resembling this word. On the other hand, the name is too close to "Wonsqueak" in the Schoodic area to be an accident; indeed, it seems quite likely that Cadillac was actually living next to the Point, probably running a fur trade post here before moving westward to establish his new post at Detroit.

The Wabanaki and their French allies were successful in driving the English from most of Maine in the 1690s, but by the early 1700s, the conflict reignited. An anchorage near Schoodic Point, possibly Lower Harbor or Winter Harbor, had become a way station between French bases along the Gulf of Maine. In October 1710, British officer John Livingstone, en route to negotiations, recorded that he was met by Baron Saint-Castin and native allies in "Casteen's harbour" near Schoodic Point ("Squeeck Point"). At this encampment, he was hosted for two days before moving up the Penobscot to Quebec. He carried news of a British victory that soon led to the French formally ceding the entire Acadian Gulf of Maine area to the English. Thereafter, the Wabanaki in the downeast region had an uneasy and usually hostile relationship dealing with steady encroachments from the English and sided against them with the French during the final conflict that ended with the defeat of France and its native allies in 1762. With the French no longer in the picture, Wabanaki people were forced to retreat to their core settlements inland or up the Penobscot and St. Croix Valleys where they live today. Their impact on the land at Schoodic is barely traceable beyond ancient middens; any burning done for hunting has been long overwhelmed by later growth and logging efforts. Wabanaki groups continued to hunt, fish and trade along the downeast coast up through the era of the Revolution, when some were willing, on occasion, to fight alongside Patriot rebels against their old enemies, the King's forces. But by the 1760s, the region was opened to English colonizing, logging and settlement, and the remote Schoodic district became part of the new colonial plantation of Gouldsboro.[15]

Furthermore: Wabanaki Names and Mariners Names—Transformed

In addition to the word that designates the Point, there are two other names of native origin in the immediate region, but all such terms come to us through the filter of English mariners, sojourners, settlers and their maps and traditions. There are some native traditions to support an origin for both terms: *scoudiac* (the burnt place) and *eskowdek* (the end). Yet in retrieving native names we are usually at the mercy of unreliable evidence from European maps, which attempted to reproduce the often distorted early visitors' pronunciations of native terms. An otherwise exceptionally reliable Royal Navy map of the 1770s, part of the *Atlantic Neptune* atlas and printed in several versions, renders the Point usually as "Skuttock" but sometimes by the misprinted "Skullock," along with other names no longer used.[16]

Another name of native origin is used by two of the land-linked islands that form the outer Point—Big and Little "Moose" Islands—using a Wabanaki word (*moos* or *mus*) whose early appearance in this name (of unknown origin) was recorded in a deed of 1848. The third native name is one that also appears on early maps and deeds: "Wannsquaque," "Winskeag," sometimes "One Squeak" and now "Wonsqueak," which traditionally designated the point east of Schoodic but now names the harbor and village region at today's park exit. As a Wabanaki term, this derives from the root *nskwe* or *wanaskwe* for "end" or "point" with an ending *ek* designating a place name and appears elsewhere in the downeast region as "Naskeag" for the point in Eggemoggin Reach at Brooklin. This seems to be the same meaning, in a Penobscot or Passamaquoddy dialect, as the Mi'kmaq *eskwodek* (with the *eskwe* root) for "the end" at Schoodic. Both adjacent promontories represented the same kind of navigational barrier to native watercraft.[17]

At some point, the Wonsqueak name was hijacked from its original context and compounded into a local folk legend. As reported by the local journalist Jonas Crane in the 1960s, the name gets an "explanation" in a jocular anecdote remotely preserving the notion of a native origin. In this tall tale, the stereotypical tragic "Indian princess," unfaithful and so stabbed and pushed out of a canoe by her betrayed lover, is said to have given just "one squeak"—or "one screech"—before drowning. Reducing this legendary utterance to a monosyllable, the harbor's name has at times been locally rendered simply as "Screech."[18]

The Wabanaki-derived names that we have show a faded native presence dimly reflected in early English maps. The *Atlantic Neptune* map is responsible for a local name of intriguing origin and spelling: "Musquito Harbor," designating what became Winter Harbor in the 1800s. The *Neptune's* odd spelling could provoke a quest (likely fruitless) for possible perversions of a Wabanaki name. By the nineteenth century, the word in normalized form was relegated to naming Lower Harbor through the 1880s until it disappeared from maps and local usage.

The harbor at Wonsqueak (with Wannsquaque—"the point," in Wabanaki—in the distance) was home to many small lobster boats in the early 1940s. *Courtesy of the late Louise Z. Young.*

Early English maps of the Schoodic Point region also used other names indicative of the mariner's point of view—the Point region as seen from the surrounding ocean. Like John Smith's maps of the 1600s, the Royal Navy's *Atlantic Neptune* map in its several editions of the 1770s introduces names likely never used by local landsmen, particularly in the Schoodic Point region. In one edition of the *Neptune* map, a cove close to Wonsqueak Harbor that now has the name (of unknown origin) "Bucks Cove" was labeled "Lobster Cove"—possibly as a source of a mariner's seafood. Today's Schoodic Island was variously named "Lamb Island" or "Lane Island"—perhaps for one of the proprietors of colonial Gouldsboro or for its potential as sheep pasture. The widest harbor to the east was named "Watering Cove" for a stream that supplied a ship's water barrels. Though this Royal Navy chart was a navigator's best resource for almost a century, the names it recorded had largely been replaced in U.S. coastal survey maps from the 1860s with names more familiar to those who lived near Schoodic.

CHAPTER 4

DEVELOPMENT AND SETTLEMENT AT SCHOODIC

With the displacement of the Wabanaki and the French, English proprietors and settlers first looked not toward outlying peninsulas like Schoodic but to the relatively promising salt marsh meadows and potential farmlands of the upper bays along the coast. Here they found ready-made salt marsh hayfields as a crucial base for livestock and farming, along with ready access to the taller timber of inland forests. Colonial English maps of the 1760s and '70s make clear that settlers bypassed almost all the seaward harbors and remote peninsulas, leaving Schoodic undisturbed and granting it an unusually long preservation in a nearly natural state. When settlers finally did arrive at the Point, its semi-isolation meant they would often live as a self-sustaining outlying community, not quite an island, separated yet slowly more connected to its neighbors.[19]

THE FIRST WAVE OF DEVELOPMENT AT SCHOODIC

By the late 1760s, some four miles north of the Point, the potential for marketing timber had attracted the earliest proprietors of Gouldsboro to establish a sawmill—but no settlement—at Mill Creek in today's Winter

Harbor. Since no roads reached this mill at the time, timber and lumber had to be floated to market for shipping down the narrow estuary that opens out of Lower Harbor at Schoodic, the location of the region's first settlement.

On the eve of the Revolution, it was unregulated timber poaching, logging and saw milling—more than fishing—that became established as a way of life and a marginal economy for the thinly populated Gouldsboro community north of Schoodic. A few years after the outbreak of a Yankee rebellion against the Crown at Machias, Schoodic Point once again became a military frontier as it had been for native warfare in Champlain's time. The British, solidly established at Castine from the summer of 1779, extended their control up to Frenchman Bay, requiring reluctant local residents to swear allegiance to the Crown. Beyond Schoodic Point, Gouldsboro settlers tried to resist and stay loyal to the Patriot strongpoint at Machias, but anarchic piracy on all sides, disguised as war privateer raiding, created endless bloodshed and suffering in the region. After years of being hammered by freebooting raiders, the region emerged safely inside the new U.S. borders and slowly began to develop a reawakening to the potential for commercial fishing out of the harbors sheltered by their peninsulas. Old and newly arrived settlers now moved seaward into the area's southern bays and harbors, closer to the Schoodic Point region.[20]

Schoodic's First Settler

Along with this shift, the first recorded English inhabitant in today's Winter Harbor region arrived at Schoodic. Thomas Frazer, listed as a "mulatto with wife and seven children" in the 1790 federal census, settled on Schoodic's west side at the harbor, creek and point still bearing his name: Frazer Point. Raising his large family before the Revolution with his wife, identified in one source as a native woman, this black pioneer had apparently settled and improved a homestead lot off Taunton Bay at Egypt Stream. According to an early deed, Frazer and his wife, Mary, appear to have sold this for thirty pounds, both signing with an "X" in September 1776. In that era of chaotic Revolutionary freebooting, they recorded themselves as living in "a place called Frenchman Bay out of bounds of any town." Presumably the family took up the Schoodic salt business late in the Revolutionary era or at least by the mid-1780s. Possibly, as Thomas Frazer is the namesake of one of Gouldsboro's London proprietors (Thomas Frazier), he might have had a

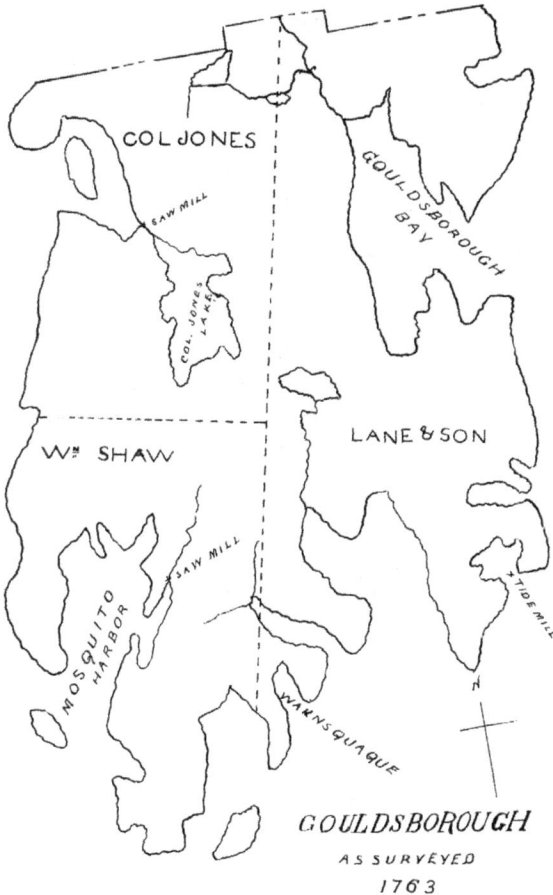

Above: Frazer Point (from the park wharf) with what is likely the Thomas Frazer house site at the top of the clearing and the Fish House site on the shore at the left.

Left: Colonial-era property map of Gouldsboro showing the proprietors' quarter sections and early ownership of Wonsqueak and Schoodic. *From* Historical Researches of Gouldsboro, Maine *(1904)*.

patronage connection that motivated starting the salt- and fish-processing venture at Schoodic.[21]

He settled at the Point on what had been the London proprietor's land, not as an owner but possibly at first as agent for the proprietor. But at the same time, he seems to have acquired a homestead lot of one hundred acres on the east side of Kilkenny Stream at the head of Skillings River. This he sold in 1799 for $1,000, enough money to invest substantially in the salt- and fish-processing business at Schoodic after the English proprietors sold out. It appears that Thomas Frazer continued living at the creek and point now bearing his name for at least twenty years, paying full Gouldsboro and state taxes through 1804 and remaining at least until 1810 after the colonial proprietary interests in the land were sold. He was occupying a spot that in time became a productive one for processing and preserving cod, and it is possible that Frazer was the first in a series of "fish-makers" using this space for processing dried fish with quantities of salt, almost all of it imported. There is a strong local tradition that Frazer operated a "salt works," providing a commodity absolutely crucial to the needs of preserving and drying cod for a growing fishery. It seems doubtful that in this small mudflat creek at Lower Harbor he could produce much salt by evaporation or even boiling, but he certainly could store imports from Britain and Portugal and refine a large amount of cruder rock salt, making it suitable for processing fish.

This early traffic in logging for a nearby sawmill and salt processing for a rising fishery created the beginning of land clearing and development in the Schoodic area around Lower Harbor. They were indicators that the pressures of national and international marketplaces were about to bring newly visible changes to the Schoodic landscape.

SCHOODIC'S FIRST TYCOON DEVELOPER

Following the chaos of the Revolution, logging and timber poaching in Gouldsboro brought a turmoil of disputed land claims throughout the township. The confused state of its land titles and squatters' claims were brought into order and stability by the intervention of an enormously wealthy proprietor whose land boundaries permanently influenced the town and the land at Schoodic. The Philadelphian William Bingham, one of the richest men in America and eventually a London resident, was among the most ambitious of the entrepreneurs to pursue heavy international investment in land development in the new Eastern Maine settlements. Bingham emerged in 1793 from a complex series of negotiations to become the owner of a vast territory. His holdings of over 2 million acres included most of the eastern interior woodlands of Maine and, as an outlet on the coast, most of today's town of Gouldsboro, along with parts of Lamoine, Hancock and Mount Desert Island.[22]

Bingham's comprehensive 1798 town survey, as mapped by Isaac Coolidge, embodied his grand design for assigning value and land development potential throughout the town. Gouldsboro's later land development was entirely shaped by his plan, as suggested by the modern survival of most of his property lines today (see the map in Chapter 2). His lots, sold off rather than rented, were sometimes bought with future-option payments on promised purchases or installment payments or complex mortgage deals, as well as outright cash. Bingham's survey plan had the effect of assigning a role for future development in most of the land throughout town and established a thoroughgoing market appraisal of its real estate, including the land at Schoodic Point. Relatively developed shore lots at the head of the bay near the center of the town's colonial settlements soon went for four to five dollars per acre; shore lots at newer harbors went for half that, and undeveloped and remote shoreland went for one dollar per acre or less—prices that largely held for Schoodic Point when its lots were eventually sold.

The lands that Bingham laid out at Schoodic presented something of a microcosm of the development prospects for the entire region. His survey plan for the Point region became absolutely definitive in shaping the dimensions of land that in time became Acadia National Park's holding. It also shaped the immediate surroundings of the broader Schoodic Point region with its Birch Harbor Mountain forest terrain. Bingham mapped out a huge lot (over three thousand acres) in the hilly area north of the original park, the Schoodic Woods, which remained a nearly uninhabited green band linked to the outer Point. This became a vast unbroken timber resource that included the watershed off Birch Harbor Mountain ridges to the old sawmill and Mill Creek in modern Winter Harbor on its western side and to Wonsqueak Bay on its eastern side, along a line defined by an old colonial quadrant boundary. This large section of the Point region remained unsold for almost a century, in time passing through various hands to create uncertainties for the twenty-first century to unravel.

For the Schoodic Point region, the 1798 survey shows a representative mix of land ownership and values. Bingham or his agents apparently chose the remote western shore of the Point to locate one of the "Public Lots," state mandated for support of clergy and education. He seems to have placed the lot in an out-of-the-way spot, but locating it here made its bounds a key reference point for properties elsewhere in the Schoodic Point region, and in time, the public lot became a determinant for Acadia National Park's Schoodic District bounds. Meanwhile, previously settled properties such as Frazer's dwelling were excluded from Bingham's purchase, so this earliest house lot, actually owned by the heirs of the colonial proprietors, was sold in 1805 not to Bingham but privately to his land agent, General Cobb. As for the Bingham-owned tracts at the Point, none was less than one hundred acres, substantially larger than most other nearby shore or harbor lots. The entire outermost Point and mountain was lumped into a thousand-acre-plus lot apparently not considered very habitable land. However, despite Bingham's ambitions, the layout of remote land at Schoodic never attracted any investment, development, permanent residence or purchase until the 1830s—quite late in the growth of the surrounding township.

The marginal physical features and skimpy resources that Champlain had identified for remote Schoodic were becoming gradually more attractive for Maine investors and developers in the early 1800s. North of Schoodic, old settlers and newly arrived war veterans had taken up land closer to deeper waters in pursuit of harbors for fishing and even whaling, forming shoreline villages that were linked with town roads by 1818. By the 1820s, harbor villagers and shore residents had slowly developed three economic conditions necessary for settlements to prosper. The region needed a critical mass of local sea fishery talent with maritime experience, along with an increasing demand for coastal timber and a steady rise in its price, plus the capital to exploit those enterprises. At the same time, a federal fishing bounty encouraged captains and crewmen to build schooners that roamed to faraway Canadian banks, amply supplying urban and southern markets with dried salted cod and mackerel. The rising price of lumber from the upper Penobscot Valley in the 1830s was driving a demand for the more marginal timber alongshore, as well as fresh sources of kiln wood. Junk wood of all kinds was used to feed the voracious lime furnaces of Rockland, burning raw limestone down to quicklime, the basis for cement. Fueling these furnaces had already denuded the nearby shores of Penobscot Bay. Buyers in an era of land speculation were now newly motivated to seek formerly neglected coastal timberland. By the mid-1830s, these conditions had ripened—even for isolated Schoodic—such that entrepreneurs from more prosperous ports in Maine were now ready to invest more than a decade of their time and treasure exploiting the resources available at the Point. Of course, their efforts had a permanent impact on the character of Schoodic's undeveloped land.[23]

SCHOODIC'S FIRST DEVELOPERS FOLLOW THE BINGHAM PLAN

The first buyers of Bingham lots at Schoodic were ready to develop both harbor lots and timber lots. On the west shore of Schoodic Point, the "Lower Harbor" at Frazer Creek and Point had already fulfilled Champlain's forecast for harbor resources. Here the land had been inhabited and probably cleared by its namesake by 1800 and possibly used by squatters for drying and salting fish in the three decades since his time.

John Frisbee's Fish Factory

It was not until 1836 that Lower Harbor's shores were purchased from Bingham and Cobb to be heavily developed for fish processing by John Frisbee, a prosperous entrepreneur from far to the west near Portsmouth in Eliot. Having invested substantial funds in ships and supplies, he set himself up in Winter Harbor at least by 1830. He was recorded in 1836 as owner of a fishing vessel, *Industry*, and in the same year bought the Thomas Frazer lot—Frazer Point—from General Cobb's heir. Within two years, he had persuaded the town to lay out a road from Winter Harbor village down to the creek, denoting the waters as "Frisbee's Harbor." It was planned to service an early resident along its northeast shore, Nathan Hammond, and cross a new bridge to Frisbee's newly invigorated fish-making facility. He began hiring crew and facility managers, including five families—three Rider brothers from Vinalhaven and two in-law families from Cranberry Isles, Leonard Holmes and Charles Norris. Soon Frisbee began diversifying, running for state representative in 1840 and, within five years, decided to pursue a medical career in Portland. He sold the entire operation in 1845 at a price indicating his large investment in the extensive buildings described in the deed. In the nine years since his 1836 investment at three dollars per acre, the price had more than tripled to ten dollars per acre (in a period when overall prices were in depression but lumber prices were taking off). A deed a half century later describes a large shoreline "fish house" here, its likely foundations still visible today.[24]

Thanks to the demand for lumber and kiln wood in the 1830s, the modest timber resources noted by Champlain had now become worth developing elsewhere on the Point. Throughout the Schoodic Point region, the scale and value of logging development during this decade is partly measurable by the price increases landowners gained on land and improvements. In 1834, a Rockland lime trade merchant, David Gay, and his partner paid Bingham the then-standard waterfront harbor rate of four dollars per acre to purchase the point and harbor adjacent to Schoodic (Wonsqueak and Bunkers). Much of the timber cut here was shipped as kiln wood to feed the lime works at Rockland. After fourteen years of logging, this harbor with buildings was sold at sixteen dollars per acre—quadruple its original cost—and was still producing wood for its new owner. Land speculation was equally evident for the formerly reserved "Harvard College Lot" or "Public Lot" of 484 shoreland acres along the sloping forested plateau northwest of Schoodic Head Mountain, bought in 1835 by a Boston merchant at thirty-three cents per acre. After considerable logging on the premises, the land was sold piecemeal in the late 1840s and early '50s at close to one dollar per acre, triple its original cost.[25]

The thousand-acre tract on the tip of Schoodic Point, with east and west mountainsides, ponds and tidal islands, was the focus of exceptionally intensive development after 1840. Bingham sold it on the installment plan to two partners, one from prosperous Blue Hill who paid one dollar per acre over four yearly stages with the proceeds from cutting the land's timber. After considerable cutting, they sold the unimproved east and west slopes of Schoodic Head Mountain in six to eight years to different buyers, approximately at cost. But the waterfront area around the West Pond was to undergo a virtual clear-cutting and considerable improvement, apparently to make it a shoal-draft harbor and logging depot. Here for a time lived one of the partners, William Roamer, probably in a log cabin like those of other coastal logging pioneers. He attempted unsuccessfully to persuade the town to build a road to his lot from Frazer Creek at Lower Harbor. To make a shoal harbor of West Pond, a "canal" or entry, still usable today, was blasted through ledges. A "breastwork" was also added and wharves and buildings erected—all shown in deeds of sale. A roadway was made along a creek to

The landing and likely wharf site in West Pond where "wood boats" were loaded with kiln wood and timber.

reach an upper clearing that eventually became a large farmstead. After nine years, the main shore lot with improvements at West Pond was sold at quadruple its purchase price, while the adjacent shore lot on Big Moose Island brought double its initial cost per acre.

Heavy Timber

The demand for wood, especially to feed Rockland's lime works, linked this first development of remote Schoodic to the lime supply and hence to the cement industry that built distant New York. The connection had distinct effects on the ecology of the Point. Because the limekilns were such continuous consumers of wood to burn limestone down to quicklime, loggers sought shoreline forests to cut intensively wherever shoal-draft boats could be drawn inshore to carry the wood. Loggers were not particular about the kind of wood they sought; anything that would burn was logged, and large areas were clear-cut down to stumps, with brush usually burned down to fertilizing ash. Such intense logging seems to have changed the ecology of Schoodic's outer islands substantially, for both Little Moose and Schoodic Islands have few, if any, trees in the twenty-first century, while they both (as shown in early deeds) were targets for timber cutting during this period. Large areas of cleared land

In the foreground is the logged and nearly clear-cut western slope of Schoodic Woods and Birch Harbor Mountain, 1889. *Photo from the prospectus of the Gouldsboro Land Improvement Company.*

on Big Moose Island, on the mainland around and north of West Pond and in much of the area around Frazer Creek are definitively shown on one of the earliest U.S. Coast Guard maps made about a generation after the major logging. Local residents recall these areas as remaining thinly forested into the 1920s, while today the varied character of tree growth here gives testimony to the heavy impacts of early timber cutting.[26]

Much of this work, apparently done by logging teams paying stumpage fees to owners, is suggested through local names that appear on deeds reserving rights to timber access or supplies. Another deed, itemizing the buyer's required payments in timber products of the land to be bought, reveals wood marketing arrangements and, by a ratio of twelve to one, the overwhelming proportion of kiln wood over market lumber: "Arey [the buyer] to pay...600 cords of good kiln wood, one half on the landing of Schoodic Island and one half on the landing of Bunkers Harbor...The wood is such wood as grows on the premises, and fifty cords of merchantable spruce wood for Boston merchants to be delivered on the landing."[27]

Lumbering was still a trade for some townsmen in 1850—as well as for one Schoodic resident, as recorded in the U.S. census—but for few (if any) in town by 1860. This suggests a slowdown of large operations in the area after the 1840s, though family efforts at firewood and kiln woodcutting continued. With few or no early roads available in the Schoodic Point region, moving timber out of the coastal forest and onto stone or boulder beaches for boat transport was certainly a challenging accomplishment. Records of early watercraft for the wood carrying trade describe shoal-draft scow sloops or schooners as well as small pinky-style schooners that could be beached or drawn up in shallow water, as on West Pond, with logs winched or slid aboard. Rockland area harbors were crowded with these small schooner "kiln wooders." While such intensive logging exploitation made for an active market-oriented trade at Schoodic in the 1840s, it produced few permanent residents.

CHAPTER 5

THE RISE OF THE REGION'S SETTLER COMMUNITIES

B ingham's plan for town development assumed that settlers would eventually take up his land plots after the big loggers had finished removing the wood. But a marginal region like Schoodic Point, with the sparse offerings that Champlain described, was unlikely to attract settlers with farming ambitions. Indeed, the Schoodic settlers of the late 1840s were not from the same background of traditional farming as were most of the town's colonial-era and post-Revolutionary settlers. Nine of the Point's new settler families combined a seafaring life with lumbering, having come from island communities farther west. Two families (Norris and Holmes) were connected to Cranberry Isles and seven to Vinalhaven, with five of these apparently linked at first to the fish processing center at Lower Harbor. By their island origins, these settlers were accustomed to remoteness and to somewhat marginal quality in available land, so the "near island" of Schoodic may have seemed an easy transition. To them, the Point region offered an attractive combination of new opportunities. Alongside the new fish processing center at Lower Harbor, the newcomers could position themselves for a profitable trade in the burgeoning cod and mackerel fishery, escaping the crowded competition of the one hundred fishing vessels at Vinalhaven. In addition, the still-standing forest offered them fresher timber than the island shores of Penobscot Bay and Vinalhaven, whose wood had been largely cleared out to feed the lime-burning kilns of Rockland by the 1840s. These families were secondary buyers of homestead property from the first wealthy developers, but their settlement followed the land division plan laid out by Bingham. His agents encouraged settlement by taking small pre-purchase payments as options for hopeful homesteaders to reserve and develop some of the peripheral lots in the Schoodic region. As the islanders settled, their families were joined by and soon intermarried with some of Gouldsboro's old settler families who had moved into the Schoodic Point region. But all the settlers were to find that the marginal quality of soil, the declining supply of timber and the restricted capacity of harbor anchorage would limit their ability to exploit the land's resources in a world market.

SALTWATER FARMSTEADS FOR SEAFARERS

If some settlers had ever hoped to develop an intensive market-oriented agriculture on the land, no such efforts ever succeeded at Schoodic. Clearing the forest in logging development certainly makes a visible disturbance of the forest ecology, but an even more long-lasting and substantial impact on a fragile landscape can occur if settlers try to develop an intensive agriculture on the land.

Lucy R. and Nathan S. Hammond, 1830s settlers at Lower Harbor. The Hammonds were later a leading merchant family and owners of Schoodic Island. *Courtesy of the Winter Harbor Historical Society.*

Somewhat ambitious farming efforts were made in three locations in the Schoodic Point region. In the outer Point district by East and West Ponds, at least two ample farmsteads were established, while in the somewhat more populated Lower Harbor settlements at Frazer Creek, another two or three operated near the fish factory. Farther east at Wonsqueak and Bunkers Harbors, early logging operations cleared land for smaller farm holdings.

Subsistence Farming

In the rough terrain of Schoodic Point, it took much effort to clear and develop such acreage in a region where even the inland farms were not very productive. Still, the prospects for farming a peninsula may have looked relatively good to these immigrants from the islands. They could certainly expect to get a good initial crop from newly cut timberland enriched by ash from burned brush—a typical slash-and-burn agriculture as practiced on cut-over ground to the west on Swan's Island. Yet the fertility on such thin soil, even if fertilized with seaweed and a little manure, could not last, as none of these farm operations appear to have been large, bountiful or intensively worked. Crops were typically limited to hay, potatoes, some oats, barley, corn, buckwheat, peas or beans. Apples were certainly important, for these trees can still be found around West Pond, East Pond and Lower Harbor. Fish and especially clams provided much protein, as evidenced by several clamshell dumps around the farms. The livestock on early Eastern Maine farms had none of the well-balanced productive meat, dairy and wool features of today's animals or even the early improved breeds of Western Maine or those of post–Civil War Maine. Their animals were old colonial breeds, the red cattle and rangy sheep of remote Maine in this era, built for strong survival traits in rough terrain. Typically, as on Swans Island, oxen rather than horses were the work animals.[28]

Town tax records are not available to tell us the specific size of Schoodic livestock holdings for this period, but most herds in the neighborhood appear to have been very small; records for the 1880s and '90s show that none of the farms in the Schoodic Point vicinity had anything more than one cow, two heifers, a horse, perhaps a pig and some chickens and up to fifteen sheep. Judging from estimates of early extensive subsistence farming elsewhere in New England, the farmers at Schoodic were operating barely at a subsistence level. They had perhaps enough to barter locally with a doctor or village merchant to feed families but no prospects for intensively farmed production for a larger world market.

Thomas Arey (the First), the farmer at West Pond, developed a relatively large field for tillage and adjacent pasture. The town agreed in 1855 to link his Schoodic Farm and landing at West Pond with an overland roadway from Lower Harbor (known in deeds as the Schoodic Road). If Arey hoped this commercial link might increase the scale of his farm by enabling farm goods to reach the village of Winter Harbor both by land and water, he was ultimately disappointed.[29]

Dr. Pendleton's Journal

A hint of the role of Schoodic's farm produce in the local commercial market can be gleaned from the journal books of a local physician and justice of the peace, Nathaniel Pendleton of Winter Harbor. His journal is the only readily available source for recorded daily life on Schoodic Point during the mid-nineteenth century, and it is particularly revealing because Pendleton's career as physician, justice of the peace and shipowner made him a frequent traveler to all sections of the Schoodic Point region.

Dr. Pendleton recorded how he took some of the Point settlers' goods in barter trade for his services during the 1850s and '60s. The Ephraim Rider family on the north bank of Lower Harbor kept enough cattle to offer milk, hay and manure in barter payments. The Myricks on the Point at Big Moose offered some building stone (though no substantial quarry is evident here), wool and apples to the doctor, while a neighbor at Bunkers Harbor traded potatoes, sheep and the use of horse and ox teams.[30]

SETTLED AND UNSETTLED SECTIONS OF THE SCHOODIC POINT REGION

Settlement in the Point region formed in clusters around usable landings or harbor facilities, leaving large tracts on either side of Schoodic Head Mountain uninhabited and devoted to logging. By the mid-1800s, the region's population reached about 180 people living off the land and its harbors.

At Lower Harbor

Frazer Creek bore a series of names reflecting its phases of settlement (Frazer Point, Frisbee's Creek, Weir Creek, Mosquito Harbor and Frazer Creek), and in time the area became the village of Lower Harbor. Here in 1840 lived a thin population of three families: John Frisbee, the salt fish operator, along with a possible employee family (Bragdon) from Sullivan as tenants and soon-to-be owners, as well as a nearby old settler, Nathan Hammond, who occupied and probably cleared a lot he was apparently buying on credit from Bingham. Five years later, with two of those families gone, a new wave of settlers had arrived along with a turnover in the salt fish ownership. The two Cranberry Island families of Norris and Holmes now became partners in the business with help enlisted from three Vinalhaven Island families, those of the three Rider brothers. Within another three years (by 1848), four more Vinalhaven families were drawn in to populate the Schoodic Point region more widely, settling five different saltwater farmsteads before 1850.[31]

At Lower Harbor, the family of Charles Norris developed perhaps ten acres of tillage and pasture south of his fish wharf operation, and two of the Rider families, his former employees, farmed about five acres with extensive pasture walls north of Frazer Creek. Today, most of these farmsteads can still be found, edged by cleared fieldstones and marked by walls, cellar holes, clamshell dumps, bridgeheads and roadwork all quite visible. Those on the south shore of Lower Harbor continue to be under archaeological study sponsored by Acadia National Park.

At West Pond

By the late 1840s, two more Vinalhaven families were clustered around the extensive clearings by the former logging landings at West Pond. Jabez Myrick, a fishing captain, had almost one hundred cleared acres on Big Moose Island, and Thomas Arey, a farmer, had even more land by West Pond under Schoodic Head Mountain. At his Schoodic Farm, Arey put

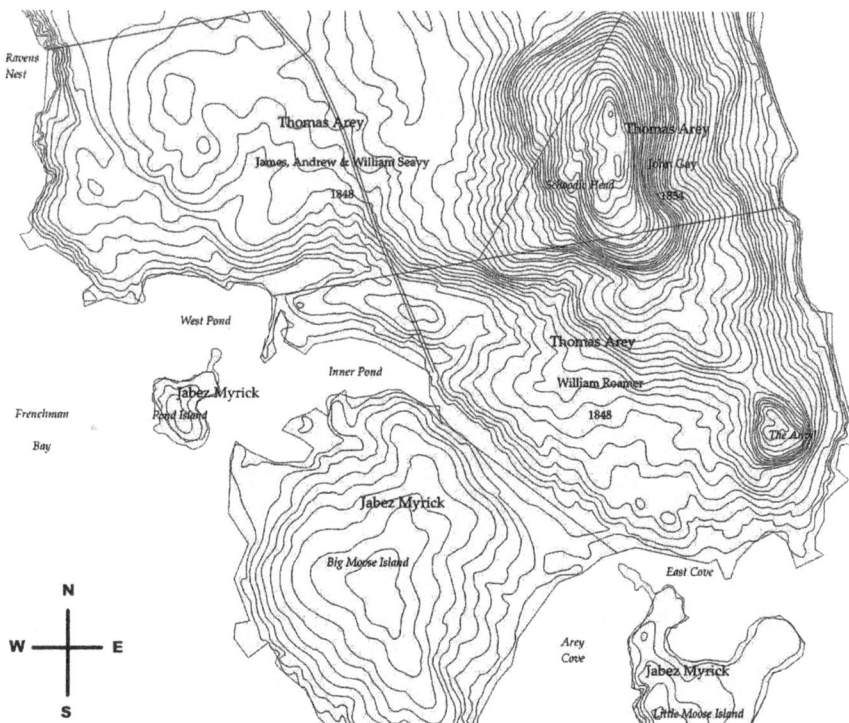

Farm settlement properties of the 1850s near the end of Schoodic Point. *Map by Thomas Mayer.*

extensive effort and investment into arable fields and pastures along with the road link from Lower Harbor, whereas Myrick's farming apparently took second place to his extensive fishing ventures. A quarter mile away was Arey's nephew James's fishing homestead by East Pond. The old fields of these farmlands can now be seen along the Alder Path trail, the terrain largely grown up in shrub and alders that provide shelter and forage for warblers and other birds rather than the former farm animals.[32]

At Wonsqueak and Bunkers Harbors

Beyond to the east, at nearby Wonsqueak and Bunkers Harbors, a closely related saltwater farming family settled in the late 1840s. Here lived the Vinalhaven cousin of the Schoodic Farm owner who, because the two cousins' names were identical, called himself Thomas Arey the Second. Probably Thomas the Second was drawn to Schoodic through his sister, who was married to one of the Vinalhaven Rider brothers at Lower Harbor. Thomas had started with a logging and fishing operation, at first centered on an 1840s purchase of Schoodic Island, and then expanded to the small-scale farming at Bunkers that eventually supported his retirement. He soon began subdividing plots along the harbor at Bunkers and inland, giving some to his daughters and selling others. By 1850, the population of the Wonsqueak and Bunkers Harbor area had grown to thirty-six people in seven families. But the other Schoodic settlements were larger by comparison; there were fifty people in ten families at Lower Harbor and another twenty-five people in four families on the outer Point around East and West Ponds. Ten years later, the two areas of settlement in the region were nearly evenly balanced, with a population of sixty-one at Lower Harbor and by the outer Point ponds and seventy at Wonsqueak and Bunkers Harbors. The ebb and flow of population and prosperity for these two areas makes an interesting contrast over the years. Those in the west at Lower Harbor and the outer ponds are relatively stronger at the start, with more ambitious farms on cleared land and an active fish processing operation. However, they grew weaker after the Civil War, while those in the west at Wonsqueak and Bunkers kept pace or became gradually stronger.

Outer Island Development: Schoodic, Turtle and Rolling

Schoodic Island does not seem to have supported full-time residents in the mid-nineteenth century, but it was certainly a busy center of commerce. It remained a speculator's investment property until 1837, at which point it was purchased by a Gouldsboro man who, in turn, had sold it to Thomas Arey the Second by 1844. Arey used the island for storing timber and kiln wood for shipment westward, eventually from his Bunkers Harbor base. When he was done with that, the Winter Harbor merchant and Schoodic Point pioneer Nathan Hammond held it, undoubtedly for a similar purpose and for picking up and dropping off commercial goods from passing coastal merchant vessels.

The largest island to the west of Schoodic, Turtle Island, had a different career, passing from ownership by speculators until purchased by a Hancock mariner, apparently to run fishing and some operations from the only landing on its north end. It appears never to have been farmed. By the Civil War era, the northern landing with its link to adjacent smaller islands made a waterway useful for trapping fish, eventually menhaden. Apparently, logging was always difficult, as the southern or seaward end was hard to reach and may scarcely have been logged.

The smallest island off the outer Point, Rolling Island, lies a half mile off the eastern shore. It might have served as a small staging for logging operations along the eastern shore of Schoodic, or it may have been logged for its own tiny two acres, but the island does not offer much for a landing. It was owned in 1859 by Jabez Myrick of Big Moose Island and George Wescott, his neighbor at Wonsqueak.

The Decline of Schoodic Farm

Throughout the 1850s, the Point region's three neighborhoods were dominated by Vinalhaven farmer-fishermen, many related by blood or marriage. However, as a farmer, Thomas Arey the First at Schoodic Farm evidently failed to make a profit on his large holdings at the outer Point, for soon after the road was built in 1857, he began seeking mortgage loans and eventually buyers for his farmstead. By 1860, he had already cut his losses and moved to nearby Sorrento, renting the farm in 1864 to Dr Pendleton's brother and mortgaging it by 1866.

The collapse of Schoodic Farm is symptomatic of the dilemma of the other farms in the Point region, which had faded or greatly reduced in scale after the Civil War era. The cause was certainly the region's thin and infertile soil. Repeated extraction of hay and crops from this ground, even if fertilized with a typical mix of manure and seaweed, would soon exhaust what struggling farmers could extract from marginal land. Operating at the outer edge of what the sparse terrain could sustain, Schoodic's farming families had to seek prosperity elsewhere.

Furthermore: Schoodic Island—A Maritime Commercial Crossroads

From a mariner's perspective, the outer edge or "point" that must be navigated past Schoodic Point is actually the ledge reaching southward from Schoodic Island—now marked by a navigational buoy. The island itself, about a mile long by a quarter mile wide, stretches due north and south about three-quarters of a mile east of the Schoodic Point mainland and Little Moose Island. The few trees on its south end today provide nesting and some shelter for the seagull colony that is now its sole population, but it undoubtedly had more trees in the past, based on deeds authorizing the cutting of wood there. Although this thinly covered island of perhaps two hundred acres seems relatively worthless from today's perspective, it continually fetched large sums—from $400 to $800 dollars—throughout the 1800s. This was approximately the same price per acre fetched by waterfront land in commercial harbors. Though its ocean exposure on all sides gives no harbor protection, a stone beach with barrier ledges on the western side faces a sheltered passage between it and the mainland; because of the ledges and stone beach, there is a relatively sheltered landing here in suitable weather. As a mariner would see it, this was the key to the island's value—its location makes it not at all remote but directly in the path of a brief stop by all coastal navigation and by mail boats passing through. The island was several times

In the 1800s, Schoodic Island (viewed here from Little Moose) was a useful depot for coasting trader schoonermen.

bought and sold in fractions of ownership, reflecting shared commercial use by multiple owners at the same time. It became ideally situated as a depot for postage, storage and transfer of shipping goods.

Schoodic Island continues to be a key navigational waypoint for mariners. As the nineteenth century wore on, it clearly became a convenient pick-up and drop-off point for freight, mail and passengers willing to sail or row out to the landing. A packet boat, usually a steamer running east and west from Eastport to Rockland and beyond, could turn to the inside passage between island and mainland whenever flagged down by customers. With this kind of commercial use, the island would have had periods of busy human activity and perhaps part-time inhabitants, though it is unlikely that anyone chose Schoodic Island as a regular residence.

CHAPTER 6

A NEIGHBORHOOD OF
SEAFARERS

Though never a mariner like his sons, Dr. Nathaniel Pendleton showed his neighborhood's typical focus on the sea in his journal entry for June 1, 1853: "At 6 a.m. left home for Schoodic Island gunning and fishing. Got home at 3…Credit [Mr.] Hill for bunch of mackerel." In his typically laconic entry (for buying mackerel), he shows how intimately connected such a landsman could be to the nearby waters and sea fisheries, even in his hours of recreation.

In one way or another, most of the Schoodic resident-owners looked habitually to the ocean as their mainstay, as a salt fish nexus—mainly cod and mackerel—had become the key to the economy for everyone in downeast Maine. Mid-nineteenth century fishermen, unlike today's lobstermen in relatively small craft, ventured out mostly in schooners from thirty to sixty tons (forty to seventy feet) to over one hundred tons. They ranged from offshore in the Gulf of Maine, in smaller or older craft, all the way to Labrador and St. Lawrence Gulf shores and off the banks of Nova Scotia or out to Newfoundland's Outer Banks in larger schooners. A typical small schooner built nearby or in used condition, owned in shares by two to six partners and crewed by families or neighborhoods, was just within reach for families in remote coastal villages and outports like those at Schoodic. Every fisherman collected a federal bounty, based on fishing effort, along with his share of the catch. This, with the low-cost technology of fish lines simply dropped off the schooner deck, gave these fishermen a decent, if hazardous, living for a small investment. At Schoodic, neighborhood schooners were

The waters off the east shore of Schoodic saw considerable schooner traffic, anchorage and at least one wreck during the mid-1800s.

owned and crewed from the 1850s on. In a typical pattern, the *Laurel* in 1861 out of Lower Harbor was owned and captained by Mark Joy with almost the entire Norris family as crew; the *Diamond* out of West Pond in 1862 was owned and captained by landowner Jabez Myrick and crewed by his sons, with the same ship changing ownership the next year using the Lower Harbor Rider brothers as crew. As was also all too common, both these captains were eventually lost at sea. Depending on how far the cod or mackerel were sought on the banks, the fishermen might be out about six weeks starting in spring. With another voyage either soon after or beginning in the fall, there might be a summer break for farming, leaving winter as a time for construction and especially for woodcutting.[33]

FISH-MAKING

The central element in the commercial marketing of fish in this era was the "fish-making" operation like the one at Schoodic's Lower Harbor, a site suitably removed from Winter Harbor village. This odoriferous process required sun-drying the split carcasses on racks while heavily treating and

"Fish making" operations—drying cod in a coastal outpost of the late 1800s. *From* Harper's Magazine, *1880*.

preserving them with imported salt, which itself was about a third of the total cost of outfitting a fishing voyage. Each marketed barrel of dried fish required about three bushels of salt preservation at sea, as well as another bushel ashore in the drying operation. Such a volume of salt clearly needed to be imported, sometimes arriving at Lower Harbor in a rock form that may have required a refining operation behind a small dam in Frazer Creek to dissolve it in seawater and dry it to a usable consistency. From the 1840s until 1857, Leonard Holmes was the principal fish-maker of the operation. He eventually sold out to his partner and fellow islander, Charles Norris, the fishing captain. Both men seem to have hired or enlisted help from fishermen laborers who rented or owned homes at Lower Harbor. The dried fish, stacked like firewood inside barrels and casks, was stowed on the decks of schooners for shipment to distribution points or direct customers. The biggest markets for dried cod were the growing cities and the southern and Caribbean markets, for feeding slave laborers. By this traffic, Schoodic's fish production helped Maine become the nation's largest producer of seafood before the Civil War. It was the fish nexus rather than land exploitation that gave Schoodic Point settlers their prime livelihood and tied them to worldwide markets.

SCHOODIC VILLAGERS IN THEIR PRIME

In this brief period between the late 1840s and early 1860s, the first Schoodic settlers' struggle to survive seemed to reach a delicate state of balance with the land. Their population stabilized at an average of seventy-five people living in what is now the Acadia National Park area. The five islander families at Lower Harbor were joined in the early 1850s by two older settler families probably tied to the fish-making operation. One of these, Oliver Bragdon, was married within the neighborhood to Lydia Arey, farmer Thomas's daughter at West Pond, but soon moved to nearby Sullivan with her family. The turnover of these Lower Harbor properties in the mid-1850s brought two replacement old-settler families headed by fishing captains-owners Nahum Stevens and Mark Joy. Shortly after, fish-maker Holmes sold out to his partner Norris, who subdivided a large portion of Lower Harbor's south bank to a prosperous old-settler couple, Joanna Bickford Wescott and her husband, William, a land investor and kin to wealthy Blue Hill merchants. And so by the early 1860s, Lower Harbor had become a mixed community of seven to eight families with their dependents, including the Riders, making over fifty people. The West Pond area with its two farmsteads had up to six families and twenty-five people before Thomas Arey rented his place and departed in 1860, leaving the Jabez Myrick family as the main resident landowners in the area. Schoodic Point's combined population was thus comparable with the nearby village of Wonsqueak-Bunkers Harbors just to the east of the Point, which started the decade at seven

Opposite: An 1870s map of Schoodic Point showing homesteads, roadways and logged areas near the end and at Lower Harbor. *USGS Chart #306, 1883.*

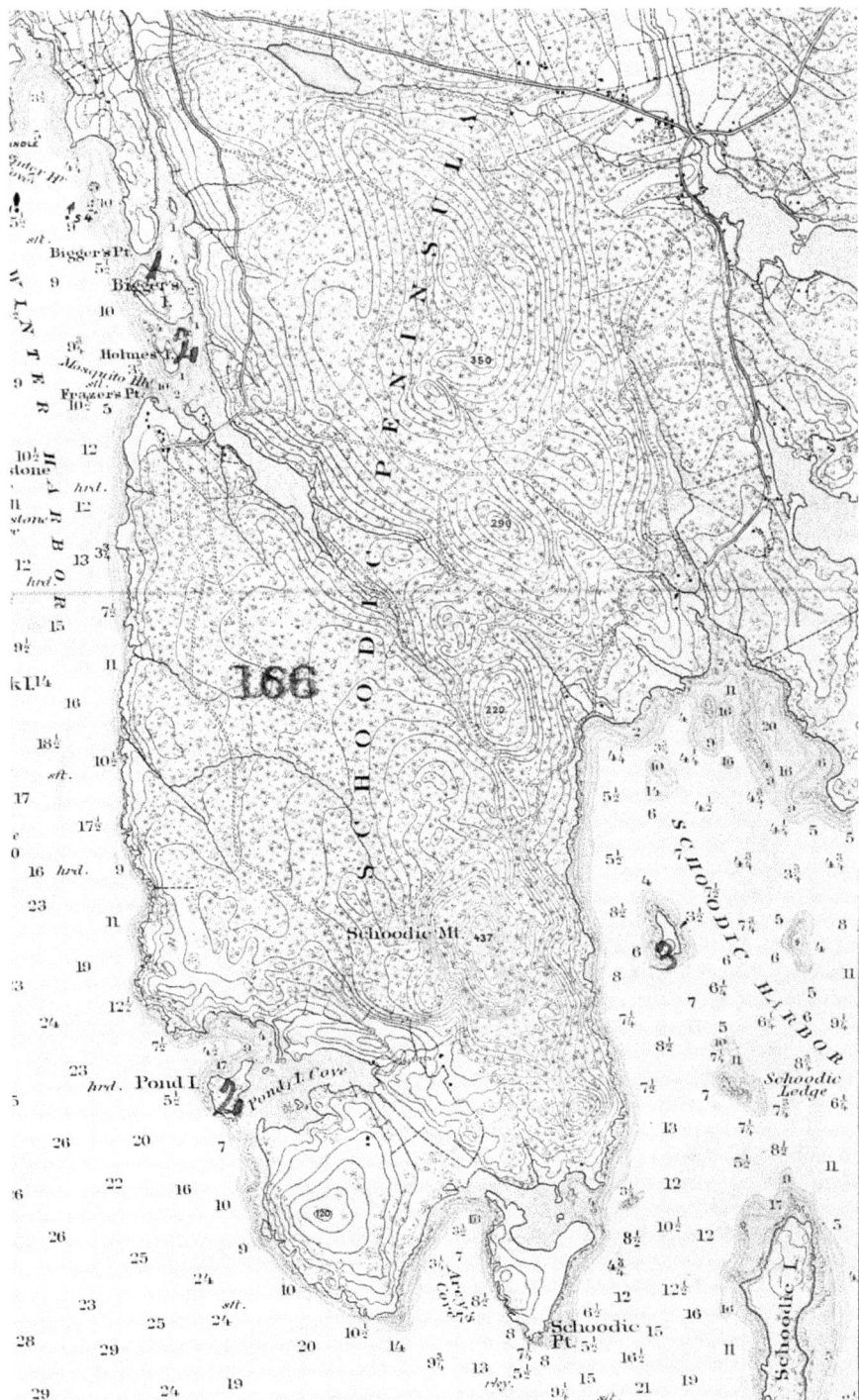

The limekilns of Rockland and "woodboat" schooner *Heather Bell*, unloading "kiln wood" cut from coastal shores like those of Schoodic. *Collection of Camden Public Library, Edward Coffin Collection.*

families and ended with eleven, growing from thirty-seven to seventy-five people. There were families settled even at the easternmost inlet of the original park, near Wonsqueak at Bucks Cove, where a son and daughter of Thomas Arey the Second made an occasional homestead. All these families were a closely connected neighborhood network in the three areas of Lower Harbor, Schoodic Ponds and Wonsqueak-Bunkers Harbors, linked by old logging roads for horse riders or buggy drivers around Schoodic Head Mountain. Dr. Pendleton's journal describes his visits by one-horse buggy from Winter Harbor to Schoodic and over the mountain to families in all three areas.[34]

Dr. Pendleton's journal during these years, when combined with census, land and town records, provides a composite view of a saltwater farmer-fisherman community at Schoodic whose social life followed patterns that might have been typical for downeast villages of the pre–Civil War era. Many lived in dwellings that contained more than one family household, while quite a few took single boarders and perhaps a majority of young couples started out life living with parental families, predominantly in a matrilocal pattern with the wife's household. A few lived in houses they did not formally own, like two residents at Wonsqueak-Bunkers Harbors who lacked land title from the Bingham proprietors and had to negotiate terms later to avoid being ousted. And though land was conventionally held by husbands, at Schoodic in the 1860s, three women acquired the family homestead property. Since traditional legal usage left widows just a one-third property interest, some of these husbands may have preferred their wives to own a bigger share outright as a form of "widow insurance." Fishing captain Jabez Myrick, who was often sued for debt, maneuvered ownership (with an intermediary) into the hands of his wife, Eleanor, probably as a way to keep his farm untouched by creditors. For most of Schoodic's owners, land was a capital resource to sell or to protect and often to leverage for financing expansion through full mortgages to prosperous men like fish-maker Leonard Holmes. For some (like both Thomas Areys), such capital was apparently raised either to purchase shares in fishing schooners or new timberland. Others, like fish-maker Charles Norris, land investor William Wescott and rich fishing captain Mark Joy, pooled their large resources to acquire almost all of the old Harvard College or "public" land as an extensive Schoodic timber lot south of Lower Harbor.[35]

A Tight-Knit Neighborhood

The complex social links in the Schoodic region are implied in a journal entry of Dr. Pendleton's: "August 26, 1855—Left home [Winter Harbor] at 9 A.M., took dinner at E. Grover's [his in-laws] at Bunkers Harbor. Called to Belinda Arey at Schoodic [farmer Thomas Arey's youngest maiden daughter]. Stopped all nite. At 11 P.M. she accused William G. Arey [her second cousin, a married man] of being the father of her child delivered at 1 o'clock." This entry epitomizes the region's interdependent social traffic, including infidelities, on both sides of Schoodic Head Mountain and between villages. In this case, the errant father, William Arey, raised in Bunkers Harbor, had already married Mary Adams, a serving girl from Lower Harbor. Kinship ties here were typically close. William had seduced his cousin Belinda while living with his wife, Mary, at Bucks Cove just outside Wonsqueak Harbor. But Mary evidently reconciled with her husband and later gave him a child of her own. As physician and justice of the peace, Pendleton was witness to all such events at Schoodic, giving extensive if laconically expressed accounts of the region's daily, pleasant social traffic and transactions of all kinds, as well as feuds, injuries and debts. This Schoodic neighborhood network gradually became incorporated into the larger town social structure through its school districts. These, dividing the area down the middle along the largely uninhabited east side of Schoodic Head Mountain, sent Lower Harbor and West Pond students into Winter Harbor village and the east villages to Birch or Bunkers Harbors.

The Deadly Plague

Dr. Pendleton's journal rolls out an especially dramatic human toll in recording the major disaster that struck the town and the Schoodic community at the outset of the Civil War. As with much in that conflict, the mayhem was not from gunpowder but from a disease that he identified as diphtheria, beginning with a few cases in the fall of 1862. Though children were especially vulnerable, young men were not spared, and there were some families, like those of Joanna Bickford, William Wescott and farmer Thomas Arey's fisherman nephew James, who lost nearly all their children. Pendleton himself survived the illness with difficulty, as noted in the entry for November 14 and 15, 1862: "As many as five or more in some families are being attacked, and may the Lord preserve us from this scourge…At home all day with this sore throat, tongue black with general disability of the whole system." The plague perhaps gave a foretaste of the loss and abandonment to come in the wake of the changing times for Maine and Schoodic after the Civil War. Interestingly—unlike those living in many Maine communities—Schoodic's people were not drawn off by war enlistments, nor were they even abruptly driven out by sparse opportunity in immediate postwar times. But the outer Point settlers were eventually overcome by sheer exhaustion of their hopes in the land and by being overtaken in their maritime livelihoods.[36]

FURTHERMORE: A MATTER-OF-FACT RECORD OF DAILY AGONY AT SCHOODIC

Daily records and journals of the past can be tremendously informative, as can ships' logs, accountants' ledgers or businessmen's records. Usually these are not very exciting to read, but they can be used to re-create an entire world. Here the journals of Dr. Nathaniel Pendleton, by naming the families he attended, give us a record of the many family and neighborhood ties that existed between in-laws, siblings, parents and children. Because of these ties, the doctor's travels took him throughout the area, especially in the Schoodic Point region, visiting family and friends as well as patients. By locating these families (by map and land deed) and noting how the journal recorded the doctor's visits, it is possible to trace his progress around Schoodic as he rode in his one-horse buggy, his main method of transportation.

However, the tone of the journal itself is quite matter-of-fact in recording events of people's personal and professional lives. Encountering such inexpressive brevity may be something of a surprise compared to so much of the impassioned writing of the Civil War era such as literature, speeches and especially emotional wartime letters. But a journal like this is largely a businessman's record—a daily reminder of "billable time"—as well as sometimes a record of the weather, travels and personal and family contacts along with those involving business partnerships and legal or political

Dr. Nathaniel Pendleton,
physician and justice
of the peace, whose
journal gives insight to
life at Schoodic from the
1850s through the 1870s.
*Courtesy of the Winter Harbor
Historical Society.*

matters. And so it is with Dr. Pendleton's journal, which is much like a ship's log—strictly the facts for the record.

Such a journal sometimes suppresses embarrassing details or even trade secrets, and it records nobody's emotional outbursts, except very briefly by the doctor himself on losing his firstborn son, Solomon, who drowned at sea in 1852. After an outburst for several days after the tragedy, his journal often mourned his firstborn at year's end in this mode: "Cold winter weather; all looks dark and gloomy; all is present but one object, this being gone forever, like the sun the light of all heavenly bodies being blown out, all is invaded in darkness, but I can only say with Job, the thing I greatly feared has come upon me."

It is worth noting how this doctor, acquainted as he was with death and disease in the community, had so many of his own children (ten!) who perished in their infancy or youth. In fact, only two offspring survived—a fearfully small part of his progeny to fulfill his hopes. This was a pervasive dimension of life in the Civil War era and before, a basic fact of life that we can scarcely imagine today.

But beyond those rare expressions of emotion, the doctor's journal is quite matter-of-fact. Here is a much more typical entry—a mix of the medical, meteorological, social and political: "My wife quite sick. Bilious fever. Boys at home. Storm and heavy gale at east. Cold. Backward spring. Fort Sumter surrendered by Henderson to the State troops."

From such cold observations, there is no direct evidence to be found here for the way people felt about their lives or one another. To tell some of the story, one must read between the lines, finding the cast of characters and surrounding circumstances, and attempt to retrieve a few fragments of the human drama that made the story of the inhabitants of the Schoodic Point region.

For example, much is indirectly revealed about the economy of the region due to the doctor's habit of taking in material goods in barter for his services. Mostly he took in basic agricultural goods or services—potatoes, hay, beans, manure, stone, the use of an ox team for lumbering, sheep or even a cow—and from this can be traced the goods produced at various farms in the region. The maritime trades are noted even more often, for Pendleton was part owner of shares in two or three fishing vessels, as was common at the time.

Perhaps Dr. Pendleton's greatest hour came during the height of the Civil War years when the entire Gouldsboro area was struck by a plague of what was called "diphtheria." He recorded its symptoms as a severe throat inflammation and fever that overcame great numbers and seemed to take an especially severe toll on children and young adults. An epidemiologist might suspect that older adults had acquired a relative immunity from some earlier outbreak, but in any case, it took more lives during the Civil War era than any other losses from the war. Dr. Pendleton rose to the occasion with frequent calls—often unfortunately with no visible relief—and eventually by providing a convalescent facility in his home called a "hospital." The doctor's great-granddaughter, in transcribing and annotating this journal, made what she called a "partial list" of those lost to the plague: twelve children in 1862 and twenty-five in 1863. At least a dozen adult deaths also appear in his journals in this period.

Such losses represented a very high proportion of the community's population in the Civil War era, and while many survived the plague, it appears that the doctors of the time were nearly helpless to slow its progress through the town. It is quite impressive that the journals record nothing of these people falling into a communal state of panic in face of such disaster. There is no evidence here of desperate prayer meetings, mass hysteria or soul-searching to affix some sort of communal moral guilt or blame, much less anything like scapegoating. The pragmatic toughness and fortitude of local people in this era is something to admire and perhaps envy.

CHAPTER 7

VENTURESOME MEN, STRONG WOMEN

Living on an outpost of coastal Maine, rugged and challenging as it must have been, was far more common in the nineteenth century than later on. The chronicle of these many outlying pioneers has been brilliantly recorded for island dwellers in the great four-volume work *Islands of the Mid-Maine Coast.* In this series, Charles B. McLane and his wife, Carol, detail the story and populations of formerly inhabited islands from Machias Bay to the Kennebec River. It provides a picture of a broad archipelago of busy coastal outposts that had much in common with nearby peninsulas—most now abandoned like Schoodic Point. In the first half of the nineteenth century, ocean transport was more reliable than anything else, critical for shipping heavy commodities like timber and quarried stone, but it was also convenient for the majority occupied in the fishing trade. Hence from the outlier's perspective, these seemingly remote spots often must have seemed quite centrally located. Because many of the Schoodic settlers had previously been islanders, especially at Vinalhaven and the Cranberry Isles, they probably found their new home on an isolated peninsula a fairly familiar and convenient location.

Some writers familiar with this outer coastal environment (such as Ruth Moore and Miriam Colwell) have reconstructed lives of inhabitants, usually in fiction or imaginative biography, and these can give a better feel for the quality of island and near-island life than historical records. But since personal records are scarce and few who lived in the Schoodic Point region were writers, only the ghostly outlines of individual settlers can be uncovered based on public documents such as census, tax, shipping and land records;

some genealogies; and the occasional journal, like that of Dr. Pendleton. The sketches that follow are based on such sources.[37]

STOUTHEARTED MEN

With most of the public records focused on men according to their households, trades, taxability or ownership, it is possible to trace sketches of landholding men's Schoodic Point careers more easily than it is for most women, owners' tenants and employees. Most but not all the men were occupied with maritime trades, so the best known are those prominent in shipping or landholding.

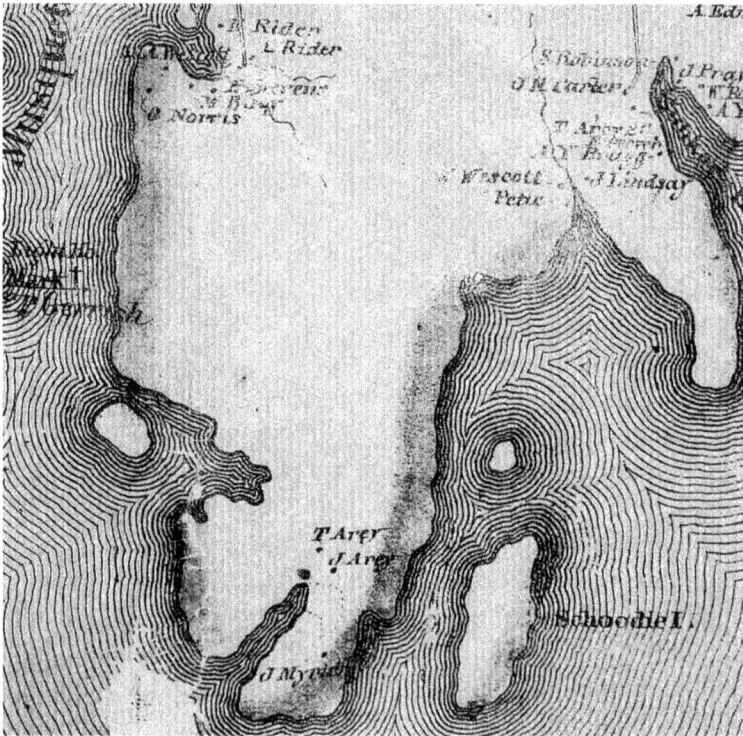

This map locates families in the Schoodic Point region during Civil War era and the plague of 1863–64. *From the "Topographical Map of Hancock County, Maine," Lee and Marsh, 1860.*

Thomas Arey (The First) (1803–1870): Farmer and Land Investor

Another islander with funds to invest in Schoodic was a native of a prolific Vinalhaven family, Thomas Arey. Because two of his relatives arrived in the Schoodic Point region at the same time in the late 1840s, one with an identical name, it is convenient to dub him Thomas Arey the First in contrast to his cousin. Born a month after his namesake cousin, he married and raised four children in Vinalhaven homesteads as "master mariner" in the island's busy fishing trade, apparently building a considerable fortune. With this he migrated to settle the end of Schoodic Point in 1848. After paying off his namesake cousin's $400 debt on Schoodic Island, Arey acquired the two largest sections of the outer Point mainland around West and East Ponds at $900—almost the same $1-per-acre price of this land before it had been heavily logged and cleared. Here he proceeded to invest further in an extensive farmstead (by Point standards) that he dubbed Schoodic Farm, with an improved access roadway from West Pond and cultivated fields over a quarter mile to the southeast of a large homestead with several outbuildings. He hired his own logger to complete the clearing, planted ground probably fertilized by ash from slash burned in logging and provided a homestead for the family of a fisherman nephew, James, at what today is called Arey's Cove. Throughout the 1850s, Arey expanded his farming operation, owned shares in a fishing schooner and developed an active role in the Schoodic Point neighborhood. His daughter Lydia married into a Lower Harbor family, and another maiden daughter, Belinda, became entangled in an affair with his married nephew from Bunkers Harbor. Meanwhile, a boundary fence dispute, probably over salt-marsh hay inside Big Moose "Island," simmered with his neighbor Myrick. In 1855, at the peak of his tenure, Arey promoted a town-built "Schoodic Road" that ran inland from Lower Harbor to his farm soon after he had bought the rest of the end-Point land to the east. But Arey was already beginning to get restless, and he began a series of land transactions in mid-decade that eventually led to his mortgaging and selling the farmstead, abandoning it to a renter by 1860 and moving across the water to the Sorrento section of Sullivan. There, near his married daughter, he and his family lived another decade as farmers while retaining an interest in islands near Schoodic. Arey's Schoodic Farm became somewhat entangled in his estate and apparently was not actively farmed after the 1870s.

Thomas Arey the Second (1803–1895):
Logger, Mariner and Farmer

The other Thomas Arey cousin formally dubbed himself "the Second" in land deeds to clarify his identity. His varied career may be typical for the Schoodic Point region, where he moved probably because his sister Mary had married Lot Rider, one of the brothers working at Frisbee's fish plant in Lower Harbor. In the mid-1840s, Thomas the Second with his wife, Almira, and four children left Vinalhaven and in 1844 purchased Schoodic Island. He apparently used the island as a depot or shipping point for kiln wood and timber that he cut by contract, some probably from Schoodic Island itself. When his namesake cousin bought him out of that debt in 1848, Thomas the Second ventured into a risky purchase of the entire Bunkers Harbor western shore. This he bought on credit in an interesting and revealing deed, using the fruits of logging there to pay for that same land in installments. In time, the scheme landed Thomas in a lawsuit with the original developer who had bought the land from Bingham, but he held on to the land to become the first settler-owner at Bunker and Wonsqueak Harbors. The land there he gave partly to his children; the rest he sold or mortgaged to raise funds to co-own a fishing vessel with Dr. Pendleton. The doctor, an in-law of Thomas's daughter, was a regular visitor and provider of care to a frequently ailing Almira. Thomas's household also included his parents, retired from Vinalhaven and contributing a pension voted them at hometown expense. Along with Thomas's part-time fishing interests, he became a small-scale farmer on the land between the harbors of Wonsqueak and Bunkers. His only son, William, seems to have been unsettled and eventually drifted away, as did four of his six daughters—but the two who stayed produced several generations of descendants still living in the region. Having remarried at seventy-two after losing his first wife, Thomas lived to eighty-eight and was buried with a headstone, paid for by local merchants Daniel Deasy and William Handy, that reads, "Here Lies an Honest Man."

Jabez Myrick Sr. (1811–1872):
Fishing Captain and Part-Time Farmer

Another prominent Vinalhaven settler, Jabez (rhyming with "James") Myrick brought his wife and a brood of children. In 1848, he had purchased the tidal islands of outer Schoodic Point: Pond Island (then called "Welches") and both Little and Big Moose Islands. On the log-cleared land of Big Moose, reached by a landing on West Pond, he set up a large farm with extensive pasture in an area later plowed under at the U.S. Navy ball field on the 1935 base. Here he raised two daughters and five sons, providing crew for a series of small fishing schooners he owned in whole or in part. These schooners, under fifty tons and usually skippered by himself, included *Shawmut* (1854), *Aurora* (1855), *Diamond* (1862), *Henry* (1868) and *Meddlenot* (1870). The latter name may have characterized his independent views; in any case, he was often in dispute with neighbor Arey over a boundary or in debt with a Winter Harbor investor. He partnered to buy Rolling Island, and when Thomas Arey (the First) moved, he bought much of that land for his children. It may have been his exposure to debt from risky ventures that motivated him to shift title to the Big Moose farm to his wife, Eleanor, through an indirect transaction. In his final venture, Jabez Sr. drowned on a fishing voyage in 1872, after which his children sold the Arey land and abandoned outer Schoodic Point for Lower Harbor or Winter Harbor, as did his widow, Eleanor.

Charles Norris (1820–1904):
Fish Plant Owner, Fisherman and Farmer

Originally from Virginia but likely raised on Cranberry Island, Charles Norris's elder sister, Mary Ann, married Leonard Holmes, from a Cranberry family. Charles joined his older brother-in-law in the early 1840s to operate and eventually co-own the Frisbee fish factory on Frazer Point at Lower Harbor. After purchasing the plant from Frisbee in 1847, the partnership appears to have kept Holmes busy raising a family and acting as fish-maker while Norris participated in fishing operations to help maintain a steady supply. By the late 1850s, Holmes gradually divested in the region and sold the plant and property to Norris, who by the early '60s was embarking

Men putting to sea while women farm at an outport similar to Lower Harbor in the mid-1800s. *From* Harper's Magazine, *1880.*

with his young son on fishing voyages. Eventually, he became owner of a schooner crewed and captained by his neighbors at Lower Harbor. All three of Norris's surviving children remained as residents of Lower Harbor during his lifetime. After the Civil War era, as the fish processing business slacked off, Charles and two other prosperous Lower Harbor landowners combined to co-own the large timber tract, the "public lot" that today forms the section of Acadia National Park south of Frazer Cove and north of the Raven's Nest inlet. In time, Charles became the senior landowner in the Lower Harbor neighborhood, a position that allowed his older son, Francis, to pull together a large package of property to sell to land development companies within today's park area during the land boom of the mid-1880s.

STRONG WOMEN

Until 1844, no married woman was allowed to own property for herself—under common law, all her property was merged under her husband's name as soon as she was married. And as a widow, she was entitled to only a one-third interest of her husband's estate, even if much of it had been hers originally. That changed in Maine after 1844, just in time to determine that many properties at Schoodic Point would be purchased and owned by newly empowered married women. Several of the women of the Schoodic Point region played central roles in negotiating the transfer of property, as well as in managing and working the homestead farm while fisherman husbands were many months at sea.

Eleanor Brown Myrick (1816–1890): Owner of Outer Schoodic Point

When the Jabez Myrick family bought the end of Schoodic Point in 1848, they settled on Big Moose Island in the midst of a logged-over area, shown along with their farm buildings on early maps. With sons aged nine, seven and five and daughters aged ten and two, they managed to build a home, where Eleanor gave birth to two more children. As her husband, Jabez, was a fisherman who captained multiple voyages every year, soon taking three of his sons with him, Eleanor Brown Myrick was largely left to supervise the farm with the help of two daughters and sons who might be ashore. Part of the farm was evidently devoted to growing apples, while other parts were dedicated to the minor quarrying of building stone and harvesting tallow and wool from cattle and sheep—all sold in payment to Dr. Pendleton over the years. Apple trees can be found on the farthest reach of what had been the cleared area, suggesting a large grazing pasture. Within five years of their settlement, Jabez lost a debt dispute with a Winter Harbor man, and two years later, the entire farm was transferred to Eleanor as sole owner, using an intermediary transaction to be sure that Eleanor's ownership was not connected to her husband's debts. In the 1850s and '60s, the farm with its family and hired hands supported between twelve and fifteen settlers on Big Moose Island.

Eleanor's children married spouses from both east and west of outer Schoodic Point. Her eldest daughter and second son married and moved to Wonsqueak and Bunkers Harbors, while her youngest two sons eventually moved to join Winter Harbor spouses. Most of her sons turned to fishing, the eldest three becoming regular fishing captains along with their father. By 1866, her third son, Christopher, had married a Lower Harbor girl and soon bought a house on the small point near the original park entrance at Frazer Creek, where he was joined by a married brother and sister, all three couples living together by 1870. The eldest sons were part of their father's land transactions, buying up the adjacent Arey farm after its abandonment. Thus, all but Eleanor's youngest children were ready to move out when, in 1872, Jabez Sr. drowned, leaving her solely in charge of the farm. She evidently found it untenable on her own, for the farm was soon abandoned to become a summer residence when widowed Eleanor married a Winter Harbor man, David Weare, and moved to town, followed by her younger sons and their wives.

Over time, the farmstead on Big Moose was divided among Eleanor's many heirs, sold to John Moore and, with the arrival of the U.S. Navy, plowed under to become a baseball field. Until 2010, an old Navy roadway leading to the site was named Myrick Road, since renamed to remove the last trace of a once-substantial settlement at the end of Schoodic Point.

Susan Coombs Rider (1819–circa 1890):
Mistress of a Large Farmstead

The three Rider (or Ryder) brothers who came to work for Frisbee in the early 1840s all brought their families with them from Vinalhaven. They all turned to fish-making and fishing and took up residence in the same section of Lower Harbor on the north bank of Frazer Creek, renting house lots from early settler Nathan Hammond. The eldest brother was Lot Rider, with his wife, Mary Arey, followed by Ephraim and his wife, Susan Coombs, and John with wife Mary. Together in the late 1840s, the three families purchased timberland on the east shore of Schoodic Point but evidently found logging too difficult there, so they sold to the Areys and went their separate ways. John's family left the area before 1860, while Lot remained and continued primarily in the fishing trade. Susan Coombs Rider and her husband, Ephraim, however, turned to farming, renting and maintaining hayfields, sheep and cattle on what had been Nathan Hammond's farmstead. Starting in 1859, they began negotiating for land, and in 1861, Susan in her own right purchased Hammond's original homestead. Pendleton's record shows Susan and Ephraim selling hay, wool and manure, evidently surplus from cattle farming. The farm seemed prosperous, for its many stonework pens are still visible. The stream that watered their land became known as Rider's Creek,

Two of Susan Rider's sons, Charley and Francis, lie buried in the only marked cemetery in the park area, on conserved land at Lower Harbor.

the family kept in good health and two of the children married locally. Then, in the diphtheria plague of 1863, two of Susan's sons were suddenly laid low. Lovingly interred north of the creek in the Point's only family burial ground, their stones remain as monuments to this farming family. Apparently by 1865, the loss made it too difficult to sustain their farm, for Susan and the family sold out, moving to nearby Steuben.

Sisters Joanna Bickford (1835–circa 1900) and Carlinda Bickford (1814–circa 1880s): Proprietors of Frazer Point

Joseph Ward Bickford, who may have dwelt at Bunkers Harbor with his brother Joshua in the early 1800s, eventually settled in the Birch Harbor area to raise seven children, three of whom became prominent mid-century

Joanna Bickford Wescott, Frazer Point owner. After losing all of her children in the 1863 plague, she left the area to start a new family in Jonesport. *Photo courtesy of Penelope Foss.*

settlers at Lower Harbor. First to arrive was his youngest child, Joanna, as wife of William Archibald Wescott, scion of a wealthy Blue Hill clan settled in Gouldsboro. Wescott had done several Birch Harbor land exchanges with his father-in-law, but soon after Joanna's mother died, she took ownership of a mortgage to her father's house lot. Then, in 1858, when her father bought back the lot, Joanna used the proceeds to buy a huge lot at Lower Harbor. She became the purchaser and householder of the end of Frazer Point, with fifty acres and about two-thirds of a mile of shore to the south. This was a large part of the original Frazer lot and Frisbee land, which she bought from Charles Norris. Moving there with her wealthy husband, her father, a hired hand and soon her brother Obed Bickford's family, she helped run a farm on this shore acreage for five years while raising a household of four children. Unfortunately, their career here came to an abrupt and very sad end with the diphtheria plague of 1863, which took all three of Joanna's surviving children, now buried in Birch Harbor Cemetery. Soon thereafter, Joanna and her husband moved away, selling a nearby home lot to her brother Obed and ceding the farm to her much older sister Carlinda.

As the firstborn in her family, Carlinda was almost a generation older than Joanna. She had married a Birch Harbor man, Lemuel Crane, who became a lighthouse keeper at Cranberry Island before moving in his sixties with her and their family to Lower Harbor as an assistant keeper at Mark Island lighthouse. Carlinda Crane and her family had taken over the Frazer Point homestead by 1870, continuing part-time farming there while her four sons and son-in-law took up fishing the local waters and possibly lobstering. A decade later, Carlinda was a widow and matriarch of the large household of sons and in-laws. Her son Elisha, who took an adjacent household of his own, drowned in a heroic rescue effort off Turtle Island, memorialized in a homegrown ballad: "In Memory of Elisha Crane of Lower Harbor, Drowned March 31, 1898."

Eunice Hamilton Myrick-Bickford (1856–1934): Landowner at Lower Harbor

Susan Rider's plague-decimated family sold their Lower Harbor farm to the Tracy family, whose seventeen-year-old daughter married Eleanor Myrick's third son, Christopher, in 1866. Christopher promptly bought a place nearby at Lower Harbor and then moved his bride into a crowded house with his two newly married siblings and their spouses. Amid this throng, the couple managed to have a daughter; however, the mother apparently died, and by 1873, Christopher Myrick had a new wife, Eunice Almira Hamilton.

Eunice, more than a full generation younger than the first settlers at Schoodic Point, presided over a large house and barn whose foundation is still visible at Lower Harbor on the small point near the original park entrance at Frazer Creek. Her husband, Christopher, had been an active fishing captain but by 1880 was recorded as living at home with a "spinal disease," which seems to have taken his life two years later. Eunice was thus left a widow and stepmother at age twenty-six in sole possession of the house on the little point and many acres of cleared pasture or cultivated land on the south side of Frazer Creek. As a Myrick widow, she had considerable land interests, making settlements for her stepdaughter in the West Pond section of outer Schoodic Point and, later, several transactions for Frazer Creek land. At age twenty-nine, she took on a new husband, Lewis, the second son of Obed Bickford, brother of Joanna and Carlinda. With this marriage, Eunice Bickford soon occupied a central role in the families of the three Bickford brothers (Charles, Lewis and Richard) and their father, Obed—the last clan of old settlers whose families filled a local schoolhouse at Lower Harbor until the World War I era. At age thirty-five, she gave birth to her only child, who died at ten months. Despite her pivotal role in the evolution of so many families and land at Lower Harbor, Eunice was to have no surviving progeny of her own. With the rest of the clan, she and Lewis moved to Winter Harbor after the patriarch Obed's death.

FURTHERMORE: SHIPWRECKS AS LOCALLY REPORTED AROUND SCHOODIC POINT

It would seem a safe assumption that a far promontory like Schoodic Point would be a formidable and famous "graveyard of ships," but local records of such wrecks are hard to find. Jonas Crane, the journalistic purveyor of local legends, passed on a tale of an anonymous English brig wrecked during a gale, leaving two of its drowned crew to haunt the shores of Schoodic Point. He cited early Point residents telling how "on stormy nights the ghosts of the sailors danced at the water's edge." Alas, the Point does not lack for drowning victims to provide possible ghosts, but rather than shipwrecked sailors these have been mainly unwary tourists washed off the outer ledge by unexpected waves and drowned before rescue was possible. A number of drowned seafarers from small boating accidents have fetched up along Schoodic's shores in recent memory, including a woman found in a tide pool near Frazer Point in 1933 and identified only by a clothing label that prompted the spot to be known thereafter by area residents as "Clara's Landing."[38]

But other local sources tell of larger vessels wrecked here a century and more ago. On November 11, 1860, at Rolling Island off the eastern shore of Schoodic Point, an unnamed schooner was wrecked, as reported by Dr. Pendleton's journal, mentioning no loss of life but declaring the ship "a total loss." In approximately the same location in Wonsqueak Bay, an early chronicler identified a wreck of the schooner *Annie McNab*, but here the wreck was reported salvaged by a local man staying with Thomas Arey the Second at Bunkers Harbor. It is hard to know what to make of these

Angry seas off the shore of Schoodic caused shipwrecks and, later, loss of life for park visitors coming too close to surging waves at the Point.

reports. Do they identify the same wreck with conflicting outcomes, or two different mishaps?

Other stories describe big schooners wrecked nearby. A Winter Harbor man told of boating with his father in the early 1920s to salvage the bowsprit timber of a large coal-hauling schooner wrecked on Schoodic Island. Since no ship timbers have been in view along the island's shore for many years, it seems likely that any such usable shipwreck remains have quickly disappeared with the help of local salvagers. The same would seem true for the report of another shipwrecked schooner, *Harriet*, run ashore on the point on the western shore of Bunkers Harbor around 1918, with no relics in sight.[39]

As these local shipwreck and drowning tales are told, their fascination inevitably catches our attention; they deserve a respectful hearing regardless of whether official sources can confirm them.

CHAPTER 8

THE SLOW FADE OF OUTER POINT SETTLEMENTS

The economy in downeast communities started to run downhill with the Civil War and its aftermath. Most significantly, both the supply and demand side of North America's sea fishery turned against the relatively small-scale cod or mackerel fishing operations that had sustained Eastern Maine communities like those at Schoodic.

The brief surge of wartime demand for Maine's salt-dried seafood was quickly negated by inflationary costs for all fishing supplies—especially salt—while postwar politics cancelled the long-standing fishing bounty, a combination that drove many small schooner operations out of business. The larger operations that survived in major ports, such as Castine, Boothbay Harbor or Portland, had capital for economically efficient big schooners and new equipment and methods. This meant seine netting or trawl lines fished farther offshore, fleets of dories and crews who were no longer fishing partners but low-wage hired help. A few areas developed the critical mass for a specialty, like mackerel seining at Swans Island and Boothbay, which also led in the fish packing industry. But small, remote harbors began to face obsolescence when large-scale and more capital-intensive fishing methods were improved, and America's changing food habits created a new market for fresh fish in preference to dried and salted. Fishermen far downeast could not supply the market to distant Boston and New York as they lacked the fast rail lines and refrigeration becoming available elsewhere. While some schoonermen in the nearby larger villages of Winter Harbor and Prospect Harbor could profitably maintain an offshore fishing operation, the shrinking

As small-scale local fishermen lost control of the banks fishery in the 1870s and '80s, they worked trawl lines just offshore in nearby waters. *From* Harper's Magazine, *1880.*

dried cod and mackerel market could no longer profitably support a small fish-making operation at an outport like Lower Harbor at Schoodic. In fact, Charles Norris, the surviving owner of Lower Harbor's fish-making center, had already by wartime evidently scaled down the operation and turned to saltwater farming, though his sons and most neighbors remained fishing, probably shifting gradually into the newly rising inshore fisheries for lobsters and herring.[40]

THE POST–CIVIL WAR ERA

By the war's end, many of the early settlers had scattered. Captain Mark Joy's drowning death left a widowed family, while other resident-owners suffered plague losses and moved away, including the Rider brothers, James Arey and the original Wescott-Bickford family. This turnover, along with the death of Jabez Myrick in 1872, motivated many of the original settlers'

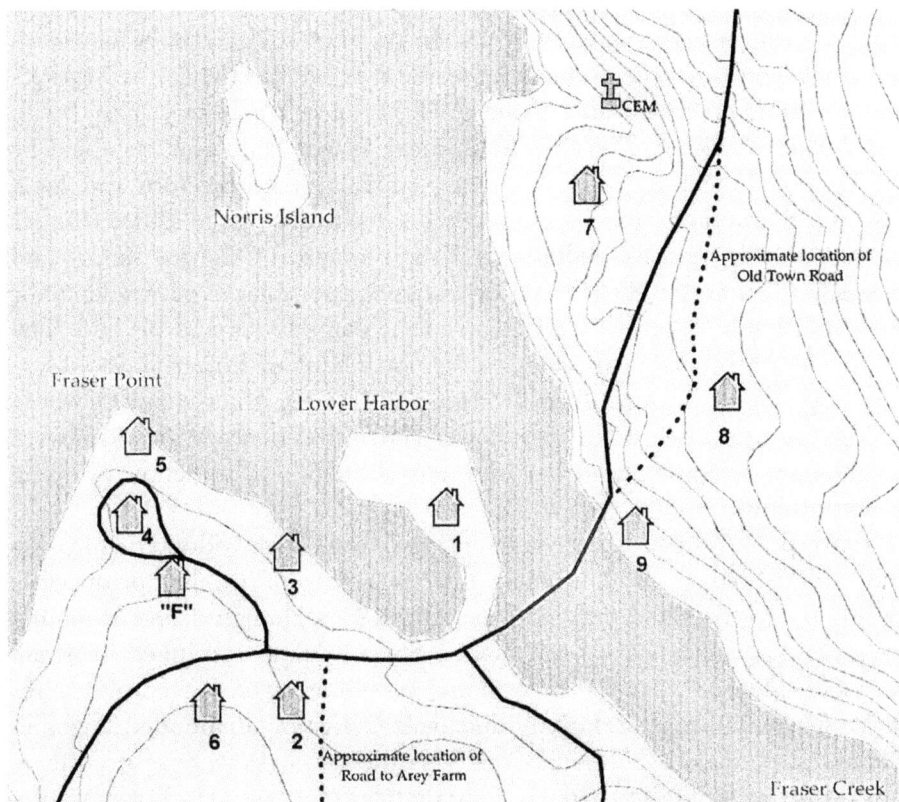

Lower Harbor houses identifiable from ruins and photos: (1) E. Bickford, (2) F. Norris, (3) M. Joy, (4) E. Crane, (5) C. Crane, (6) C. Norris, ("F") Frazer location, (7) Rider and Tracy, (8) O. Bickford and (9) H. Young. *Map by Thomas Mayer.*

children to remove to new locations in the Schoodic neighborhood. Myrick's children had married spouses from adjoining villages on both sides of the Point, at Bunkers or Birch Harbors to the east or at Winter Harbor to the west of Schoodic Point. In moving on, they gradually sold off or deserted their family holdings by West Pond at the end of Schoodic Point. The original Arey and Myrick farms in the West Pond area had turned over first to Myrick family ownership and then to an investor, eventually becoming deserted sheep pastures and wood lots. This left the end of the Point with no full-time inhabitants except for summer residents and those involved with shepherding or fishing camps.

However, Lower Harbor village at Frazer's Point and Cove remained a center for the Point's reduced population of between forty and fifty residents up through the early 1880s. In the mid-1870s, a large house on the small point in Lower Harbor became a family residence for Myrick's son Christopher Edwin and his new wife, Eunice, apparently shared with other Myrick siblings. Another house near Frazer Point was occupied by the Wescotts' Bickford in-laws and their families, Obed Bickford and, later, his sister Carlinda Crane. These related clans, with original settler Charles Norris and his married children plus the remnant of the Joy family and two other Young families, made up a tightly knit cluster of residents for the south bank of Lower Harbor up to the early 1880s and beyond. The small Rider brothers' farmsteads on the north bank of Lower Harbor were taken over by old settlers Obed Bickford and Lindsey Tracy, many of whose children intermarried with other Lower Harbor residents. Widows married neighboring widowers, and children married children, somehow avoiding incestuous links.

To make ends meet in ever-scarcer times, Mark Joy's widow tried leasing the family holding in the Public Lot to a pair of mining prospectors during the town's silver mining rush of the 1880s (though deep-cut mining trenches may never have been made). Sheepherding continued on small farms of Thomas Arey the Second and his children, on logged-over acres at Wonsqueak-Bunkers Harbors and on pastures of abandoned farms in the outer sections of Schoodic Point. Out there, flocks were rescued from predators, according to the lurid hunting tales of Lower Harbor patriarch Obed Bickford. He allegedly shot a "devil cat" (possibly a mountain lion but probably a lynx), a yarn he loved to tell around the stove at the general store, providing thrills for local children. Elsewhere at Lower Harbor, Charles Norris retired to marginal farming, another man turned to ship carpentry (Lindsey Tracy), others became full- or part-time lighthouse keepers at Mark Island off the western shore (including Bickford in-law Lemuel Crane) and everyone else continued living by fishing or mariner trades.[41]

A DIFFERENT SEAFARING LIFE

In fact, most of the children of the first Schoodic settlers managed to maintain a maritime existence. If they did not ship out to distant ports in the offshore fishery or transport trades, most of the Lower Harbor and Wonsqueak-Bunkers mariners likely turned to the newly rising inshore lobster and herring fishery that was so well suited to small craft ownership and coastal weir nets. One of Frazer Creek's many names, "Weir Creek," helps confirm oral accounts that describe how fishermen worked herring nets and seines along the creek into the early twentieth century. Although Lower Harbor's lobstermen could contain a small quantity of their catch in boxes or pens, the economics of the lobstering trade was dominated by large-scale methods of containing inventory and marketing these fragile shellfish. At the outset, the fishery was structured around new canning factories like the one built early in the postwar era at nearby Prospect Harbor. Schooner-sized craft, called lobster smacks, made a circuit to collect and transport lobsters from outports like Lower Harbor and Bunkers Harbor to factories or other markets. But by the mid-1880s, factories in downeast Maine declined as smaller lobsters were outlawed for canning and, at the same time, the tourist trade fueled a strong demand for fresh lobster. To escape the market dominance of the factories and other emerging markets, and especially to hold their local catch to gain favorable pricing, fishing communities developed ever-larger lobster compounds and enclosures.

This trend was exploited in the Point region by a local black entrepreneur named Ezra Over, who started his career in the 1870s with a schooner used as a lobster smack, carrying the catch for the factory in nearby Prospect Harbor. He bought Schoodic Island in 1875 for use as a depot for storing the local lobster catch in a large car or scow. For a year or two, he stayed with in-laws at nearby Wonsqueak Harbor to oversee this island operation, both for factory supply and the fresh lobster tourist market in Bar Harbor. Though he sold the island in the early '80s, his dealership prospered so much that in 1896, he began building the first lobster pound in the region at Bunkers Harbor. He and his in-law, Frank Huckins, ran successful early lobster pound dealerships here until selling out and retiring in the World War I era.

Lobster dealerships also emerged in the early 1900s at nearby Winter Harbor, relying on large container scows for storage like the Bunkers Harbor pounds that helped secure the economic future of these communities. But at Lower Harbor, though a suitable cove was available for building a lobster pound near the bridge over Frazer Creek, the cove was left empty until about 1924—long after all its permanent residents had deserted the area. Lacking such a pound as a community center for their trade, the nineteenth-century lobster fishermen at Schoodic no longer had the kind of economic focal point that the fish-making operation had furnished earlier. As an outport, the village was perhaps three to four miles closer than adjacent harbors to lobster fishing grounds, but this minor advantage was increasingly offset

This view westward from Birch Harbor Mountain shows a highly retouched glimpse (left) of Lower Harbor in 1889. *Photo from the prospectus of the Gouldsboro Land Improvement Company.*

One of the last houses at Lower Harbor, 1932. *Courtesy of National Park Service, Acadia National Park, Motor Road Construction Reports.*

by newly motorized fishing craft and the nearby conveniences of the large village of Winter Harbor.[42]

Thus by the mid-1880s, the second generation of Schoodic settlers, having exhausted or lost almost all the economic attractions that had first drawn their parents to the land, were beginning to leave. The decline of farming on the marginal land, the loss of the banks fisheries to bigger ports and more centralized marketing for the herring and lobster fishery all drew the children of the first settlers in slow stages toward better opportunities away from Schoodic. From eight households and just under fifty people at Lower Harbor in 1880, the village dropped abruptly in size when some second-generation Myricks, Norrises and Cranes moved into Winter Harbor or elsewhere.

Lower Harbor in 1890 was down to six families: Obed Bickford and his two sons, a Joy heir, a Myrick granddaughter and Charles Norris plus two sons and a grandson, Elisha Crane, who later drowned in a lifesaving attempt. The Public Lot timberland to the south of the village, once cooperatively owned, was subdivided between the Norrises along the shore and Mark Joy heirs inland. The latter proceeded to sell small wood lots on the shoulder of Schoodic Head Mountain to nearby residents, after which they mortgaged or abandoned the rest and moved away. By 1900, Obed Bickford's extended family, with a son on Lower Harbor's north bank and two sons on the small point of its south bank, were the only recorded residents left at this formerly populous village; they hung on until the World War I era, when the patriarch died. At the turn of the century, Schoodic Point had come to be characterized locally as "unused" territory, but by then, there were other forces at work to disperse the residents from the land.

FURTHERMORE: SHEEPHERDING AT SCHOODIC

In the rough and ledgy terrain of the Schoodic Point region, a perfect match between the need for agricultural productivity and the challenge of the area's difficult, barely tillable "Schoodic soil" seemed to be the herding of sheep. And the early settlement of the Schoodic region coincided with a surge of wool culture in Maine during the 1840s and afterward, when sheep were seen quite appropriately as "forerunners of the plow" for their close-cropping tendency to churn topsoil and suppress surface growth. Older and rangy, rugged breeds were favored for their bulky wool over the newer and more refined Merino or Southdown strains. In recent times, sheep have been confined on an island, but earlier they were fenced onto the ends of peninsulas like Schoodic or at adjacent Wonsqueak, where they could forage the landscape and be relatively well protected by nearby farms with little or no care by the shepherd. In winter, sheep could be sheltered in the same area by a crude shed or fold, whereas in later spring they could be conveniently sheared for wool. The intensely churned and urine-soaked acidic soil in such a shelter has been known to resist forest growth for several generations, and the foliage and tree growth for entire peninsulas has been held in check for scores of years by these close-cropping animals. Tax records and deeds show that farms in the Schoodic area kept small herds—from four or five to ten or fifteen head—and pasture rights were conveyed along with land transactions, showing the importance of sheepherding in the region.[43]

However, to the land preservationist sensitive to a balanced natural ecology of soil, plants and animals, domestic sheepherding has been regarded as anathema. Some of the earliest writing by the famous apostle of wilderness preserves, John Muir, developed the sheep theme as a metaphor for the destruction of natural harmony. He contrasted the dirty and destructive "hoofed locusts," the "half-alive" domestic sheep that disrupted ecological balance, as against the bold fine-fleeced wild sheep that blended with the beauties of the Sierra. Certainly intensive sheepherding has long been blamed for erosion and chemical imbalance in soil, and sheep droppings introduced to a new environment can bring invasive plants that grow out of control, as happened recently on Marshall Island preserve in Blue Hill Bay. Sheepherding in the Schoodic Point region faded out in the very early twentieth century. How extensive or long lasting its impact has been here would be interesting to determine, but it is possible that the relatively small subsistence level of herding at Schoodic has enabled the damage to be absorbed into a recovering natural environment.

CHAPTER 9

SCHOODIC ENCOUNTERS THE RESORT MARKET

The growth of outdoor recreation for postwar city dwellers, as part of a nationwide desire for refuge from rapid and dense industrialization, quickly became a demand to acquire wild and "undiscovered" terrain and natural curiosities. As rising business and professional people witnessed the disappearance of undeveloped or wild land, they began turning rather nostalgically toward nature, perhaps for a sense of redemption or fresh conquest—or simply for rest, recreation and escape. What soon developed was an accelerated market demand for recreational land. On the Maine coast at Bar Harbor, the demand for resort and summer cottage property abruptly surged after the mid-1870s depression, and by the '80s, the market—perhaps following landscape fashions—was eagerly seeking high forested ground with noble views overlooking the ocean in the nearby or middle distance. By 1884, as rail and ferry service made Mount Desert Island still more accessible and developers ran out of suitable sites, it could not be long before their gaze led them eastward, even to Schoodic.[44]

A LAND BOOM IN THE SCHOODIC REGION

The market for vacationland in the Schoodic region seems to have been sparked into life in the mid-1880s, when E.J. Hammond, a successful

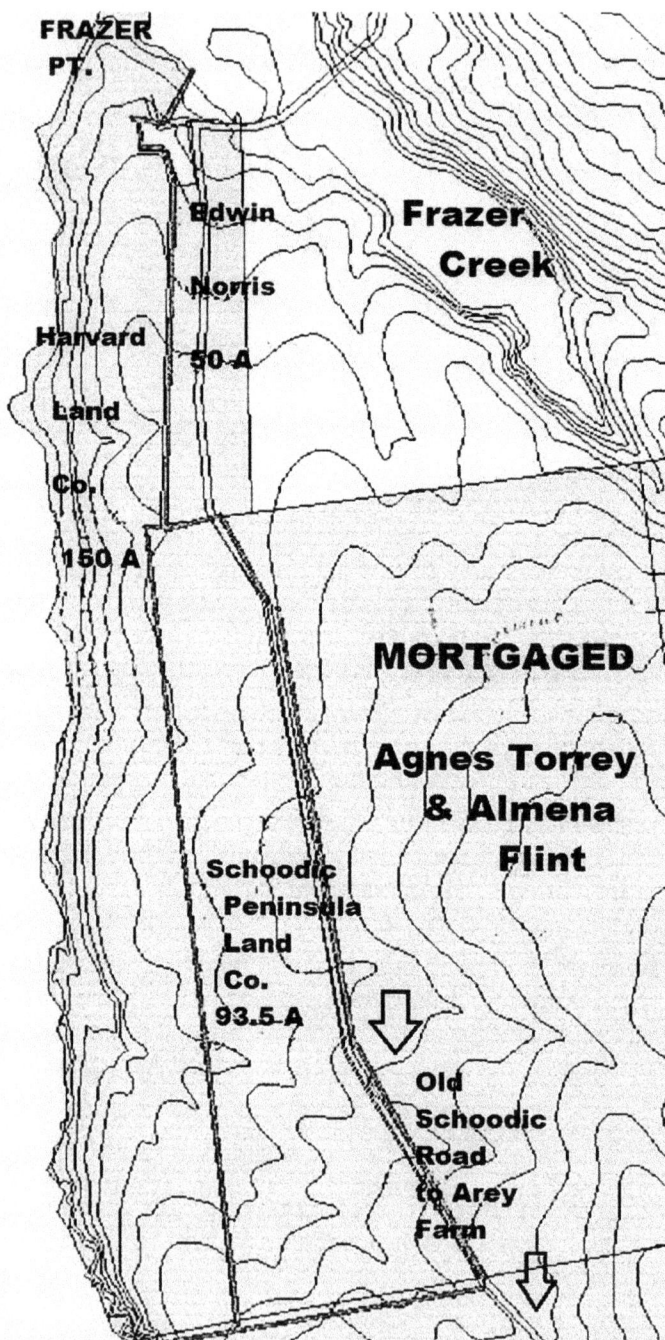

Holdings of the two resort development companies at Schoodic in 1890. *Map by Thomas Mayer.*

younger son of former Lower Harbor settler Nathan S. Hammond, made a dramatic summertime return with his family to his hometown of Winter Harbor. By 1887, E.J. had completed his purchase of prime harbor land from Dr. Pendleton's heirs, opening a resort hotel there the next year and initiating a cottage development scheme north of Winter Harbor village. This turn of events seems to have set off an explosion of vacationland purchases throughout Gouldsboro and into the Schoodic region. In that same year, local land speculators—perhaps inspired by a land boom in Bar Harbor—began extensive series of purchases in the region, with two concentrating in the Point area. Farmer Lindsey Tracy sold off the former Rider farm on the Lower Harbor north bank to land speculator Charles C. Hutchings, whose holdings soon included the land that became the enduring summer colony at Grindstone Neck. And the land surrounding the original park, the extensive three thousand-plus acres of Schoodic Woods that ran along Wonsqueak Bay, was suddenly bought from the Bingham proprietorship by Luere Deasy and combined in two years with Hutchings's lands. Within another two years, these were merged with other properties into a great New York and Philadelphia consortium—the Gouldsboro Land Improvement Company—of which both men became principals. Its holdings, clustered around the new Grindstone Neck resort colony, soon constituted the principal territory for what would become the new township of Winter Harbor. Down on outer Schoodic Point, Charles Norris's son Frank G. had already begun a series of land title clearances, purchases, consolidations and sales. Norris's selloff soon led to the creation of two large land development company holdings there—the Schoodic Peninsula Land Company and the Harvard Land Company, both based in Bar Harbor. The Harvard Company formed first and held a long strip of prime shoreline that ran from the steep banks of Raven's Nest in the Public Lot northward to land at Frazer Point sold by one of Myrick's sons. The Peninsula Company held a strip of higher ground just inland but with the advantage of direct access by the "Old Schoodic Road" track that had led from Lower Harbor toward the abandoned Arey farm. The Peninsula Company was quite active in promoting its properties, based on an ambitious development plan drawn up by another Hammond brother. The would-be resort sported lanes and avenues with names like Park Avenue and Raven Street, the latter named after the spectacular Raven's Nest bluff and canyon at the south end of the property. Several lots were sold to hopeful vacation homeowners by the early 1890s, and so in the space of less than five years, much of Schoodic Point was en route to becoming a major resort area.[45]

SCHOODIC'S SECOND TYCOON DEVELOPER

Much as William Bingham a century before had created a stabilizing plan for the town, in 1889, a group of wealthy New York and Philadelphia "rusticators" created the Gouldsboro Land Improvement Company (GLIC), which, in the Winter Harbor and Schoodic regions, imposed order and predictability upon a land development environment that was becoming chaotic. From its holdings just across the bay from Schoodic, GLIC founded the burgeoning Grindstone Neck summer colony as a private fiefdom away from the increasingly commercialized tourist world of Bar Harbor. In less than a decade, the company's holdings virtually defined what became the new township of Winter Harbor as a support and tax refuge for the colony. Through an elaborate prospectus, GLIC promoted the new Grindstone colony, announcing, among other things, its high degree of ownership and control over surrounding land resources in the Winter Harbor and Schoodic region. The prospectus stressed how the company held key resources: a water supply by holding the immense Birch Harbor Pond, a mountain lot surrounding Schoodic, uncluttered views facing the Grindstone colony and control of future development by holding land along the west shore of the broader Schoodic Point region. While the prospectus made only disdainful mention of a proposed rival development by E.J. Hammond, the company could well have had serious concern for the fate of land at outer Schoodic Point. There, while a small remnant of the descendants of early settlers was clinging to the rim of Lower Harbor, much acreage was under threat of development by the Schoodic Peninsula and Harvard land companies, who had all the appearance of "wildcat" resort promoters. And in late 1895, another mammoth resort project by two Belfast developers was being launched a dozen miles to the east on the long promontory at Petit Manan Point. The Grindstone founders' awareness of the pressure for such development in their neighborhood would certainly help motivate them to make a move on Schoodic Point.[46]

JOHN G. MOORE

A principal leader of GLIC and Grindstone colony—and, by most accounts, its main architect—was the capitalist tycoon John G. Moore. A native of nearby

Steuben, he had emigrated and developed into a major player in the harshly competitive world of New York's high finance, telegraphing and railroads in the post–Civil War era. Moore's formidable achievements included sponsoring a mid-1890s Supreme Court repeal of early federal income taxes (which waited until 1913 for a constitutional amendment) and developing a new railroad line for coastal Eastern Maine. This powerful capitalist soon established his place at the colony in a palatial new cottage named Far from the Wolf, in reference to his prosperity and perhaps to its remove from Bar Harbor or Wall Street "wolves." Here Moore entertained the rich and powerful, such as Republican kingmaker Mark Hanna and Speaker of the U.S. Congress Reed, and was reported as the social success of the 1896 season. From his huge yacht *Sachem* and the end of the colony at Grindstone Neck, Moore could look eastward across the bay to 440-foot-high Schoodic Head Mountain and Point, a view with an objective worthy of his acquisitive talent and energy. John Moore's exact motives in his 1897 Schoodic project, as reported later in newspapers, seemed to be an odd mixture of grand designs for development, purely private ambitions and public-spirited benevolence. He apparently expected his Schoodic improvements to become a major boon and amenity for the new Grindstone colony, and in time his efforts were reported to have "put the colony under his obligation." Even before Moore's purchases were completed, an 1890s town property map telegraphed his well-known intentions and virtual ownership by emblazoning his initials on Schoodic Head Mountaintop: "J.G.M." Whatever the extent of his true desires, Moore moved quickly and decisively on Schoodic Point with the immediate aim of constructing a new road to the mountain and beyond.

In early 1897, Moore began to assemble a property at outer Schoodic that would determine the shape of the future Acadia National Park property there. Working mostly through a local agent, Robert G. Davis of Steuben, Moore proceeded to bargain with the various owners, buying out the original land companies and their customers. During the same period, Moore was also busy "pulling together…a railroad combination" to finance the new railroad line for coastal Eastern Maine from Ellsworth to Calais. As his Schoodic acquisitions came together, it was clear that he intended to build a road to the top of the mountain. By the fall of 1897, he had in hand over two thousand acres, almost all of today's Acadia National Park land, and began building an entirely new carriage road about twenty feet wide along the Schoodic shore and to the summit, completed in 1898. The *Bar Harbor Record* sent an excited reporter in late fall to describe the road, which would "without doubt become a favorite drive with the summer visitors." The journalist, enthralled

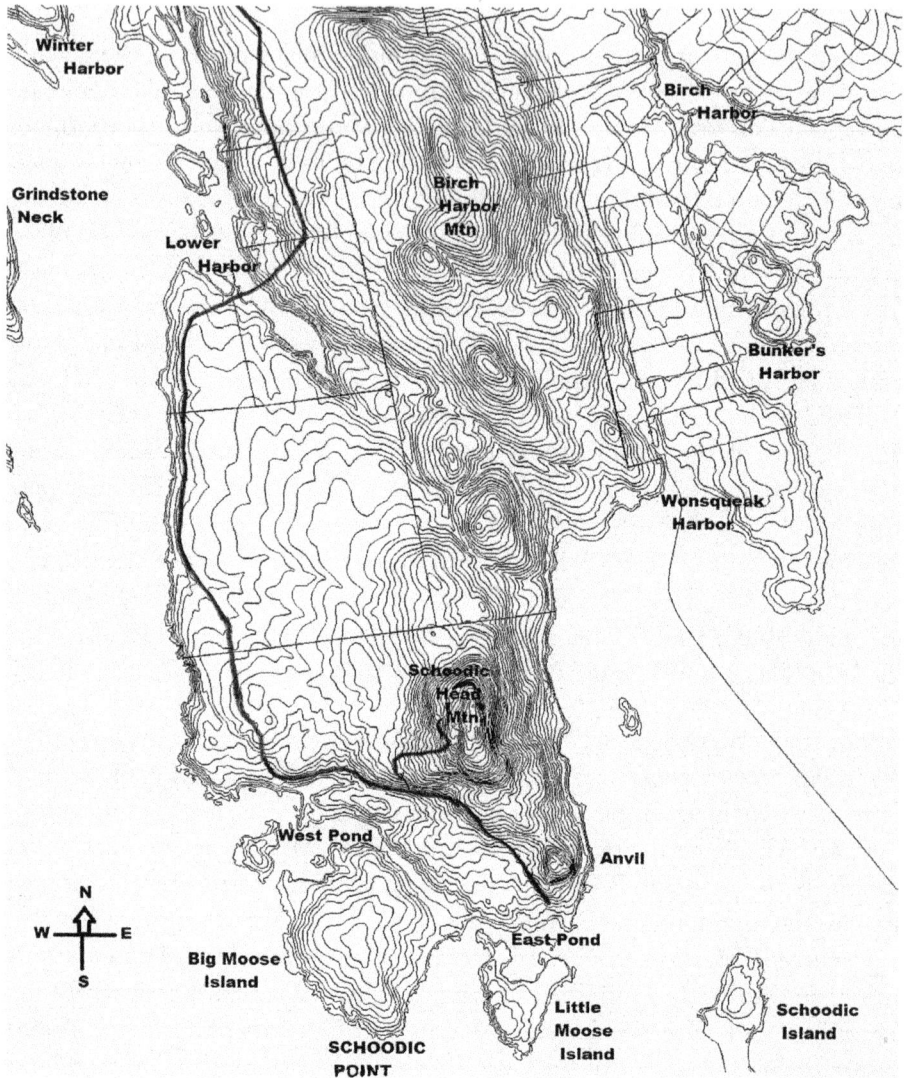

Moore bought all subdivisions of original lots south of Lower Harbor and Frazer Creek and then built his carriage road as shown. His lots defined what became the national park. *Map by Thomas Mayer.*

by the beauties of Schoodic, gave out details about a "proposed camp," evidently on the site of today's Schoodic Head parking area, which "will be 44 x 88 feet and will have a stable in connection with it." This "camp" never materialized and may have been the first of several speculative stories the reporter gleaned from Moore's followers. By the following February,

John Noonan's crew of one hundred men was part of the local labor force hired by Moore for his carriage road. *Photo courtesy of the Gouldsboro Historical Society.*

when Moore separately acquired the Moose island cluster, another excited *Record* reporter detailed plans for Moore to use the islands as "hunting and fishing grounds for himself and his guests." Details for the islands were floated "for a hunting lodge…of stone, 83 feet in length, 30 feet wide, and two and a half stories high" with "accommodations for thirty guests" and "grounds…beautifully laid out." The reporter speculated that "Mr. Moore will probably lay out over $70,000 in improvements on Schoodic Peninsula and these islands"—about $2 million in early twenty-first-century dollars. Whatever the credibility of these reports, they strongly indicate a purpose more recreational than residential, and clearly as an amenity for fellow rusticating guests to enjoy. Moore seems to have envisioned a private park preserve rather than a commercial lodge or new resort colony.[47]

Moore and his Schoodic parkland seemed to have acquired a near-mythic public role for his down-home philanthropy. The author of a fall 1898 article titled "King of Schoodic" portrayed Moore as celebrating his local Steuben origins by "buying up everything he had admired when a boy." This included "a couple of mountains which he used to contemplate from the doorstep of his father's farmhouse as ideals of the majestic in nature." Of his Schoodic purchases, the article observed: "The natives look upon the transaction as the great freak of a rich man…[while] the summer boarders from the city suspect him of indulging in some great land speculation, and are talking of the great piles of money he is going to make by cutting his 20 thousand acre pine forest into villa sites." The article went on to print what was claimed to be John Moore's statement for the press:

I bought these mountains and this land for a number of good reasons, just as other people buy pictures or pieces of china or diamonds or fancy horses. I bought them because I admired them as a boy, and it is a great pleasure to feel that they are mine. They didn't cost as much as many pictures and some horses, and they can't be stolen or burned up or die. This is the only place on the Atlantic Coast where the mountains come down to the sea, and therefore I own something that nobody else has or can have, and I believe that I enjoy the possession of that promontory (meaning Schoodic Head) as much as Mr. Marquand enjoys his pictures or Mr. Bonner his horses. There is nothing I admire more than a mountain, especially when an ocean goes with it. In the second place, I have had three years of solid enjoyment buying up that land. It was mostly in small tracts belonging to the old families in this section, who seldom sell anything but love to trade. I'm a Yankee myself and was brought up among them; thus, in buying this mountain, I have sharpened my wits against theirs and it has been a most interesting and amusing experience. It has taken my mind off my business cares, and the diversion has been worth all the money I have paid out.

Then it is a good investment. I don't expect to make any pecuniary gain out of it, but the land will grow more valuable every day. It is the finest summer climate in the world, and some time there will be a large community on that island (meaning Big Moose Island). You know that the land on which Bar Harbor now stands was once sold for 50 cents, and now a villa site costs $10,000.

I built a road to the top of that mountain (Schoodic Head) first for my own pleasure and convenience, so that I could enjoy my kingdom, and second, to stimulate local enterprise. The result is already apparent. The effect has been to inspire the authorities to improve the public roads all over the section. I showed them how it could be done with economy, and they at once saw the advantages. As an object lesson in road building it was worth all it cost. Furthermore, I never enjoyed anything more in my life than the construction of that road. It is nine miles long, and I enjoyed every foot of it. It was an entirely new experience. It did me and my family as much good as a trip to Europe, and didn't cost any more. Besides it gave employment to a large number of people who need the money.

Moore, on the basis of these words, was clearly very aware of Schoodic's potential for resort development but was apparently determined to forgo that chance, preserving his mountain for itself and for its recreational value to himself and friends. Yet his main emphasis was pride in his carriage road

The approach to Moore's bridge at Frazer Creek plunges downhill off a slope north of the modern causeway, 1932. *Courtesy of National Park Service, Acadia National Park, Motor Road Construction Reports.*

as a unique new accomplishment. Breaking new ground along the shore, he had created a roadbed that, some forty years later, was followed almost exactly by Acadia National Park engineers. Starting with a new stone-and-wood bridge over Frazer Creek (still partly visible today), the road reached southward along the shore and then overland and down to West Pond, where it veered eastward up a creek and inland past the 1855 "Schoodic Road." From here, a branch was built upward (forming a foundation for today's road) winding over abutments and a tramway on the west face of Schoodic Head Mountain to a landing near the summit facing west—the apparent site for the reported "camp" near the summit. In a second phase, possibly in 1898, another branch of the road was extended to reach a viewing place for what became known as the "salt ponds"—East and West Ponds. This branch led past the site of Arey's former Schoodic Farm and southeastward near the "Anvil" and down to a viewpoint overlooking East Pond, a track now in use as the Alder Path to today's overlook at Blueberry Hill. Moore was widely praised locally for creating a model road that gave much gainful employment for nearby town workers and also "opened and beautified the unused Schoodic Peninsula."

Did Moore Have Plans for Development?

Moore soon afterward made another important Schoodic land transfer when, early in 1899, he helped liquidate the Gouldsboro Land Improvement Company and bought most of its holdings. In the process, he absorbed the vast Birch Harbor Mountain watershed territory of perhaps 3,400 acres, including the hilly forested green band of Schoodic Woods just north of the original park that defines the peninsular character of the region. This land constitutes most of the foreground view that he and today's visitors would see from his mountaintop. It might never be known if Moore planned to include this acreage that surrounds the original park area as a unified part of his Schoodic Point holding. In fact, this section met with a much different fate from that of the future Acadia parkland he had originally secured for his roadway. While there is much reason to believe that Moore had grandiose ideas of what might become of his Schoodic Point holdings, it is difficult to assess his actual plans or intentions or separate these from what is known of him by his considerable reputation as entrepreneur and philanthropist. Gossip columnists from Gouldsboro and Winter Harbor were unlimited in

John G. Moore, a powerful financier originally from Steuben, was a Grindstone colony founder and the second plutocrat to shape the land at Schoodic. *Courtesy of the Winter Harbor Historical Society.*

their expectations. One of them supposed that with his new ownership of the improvement company's land, "it is expected that he will do everything necessary to improve the property" and that Moore might even build a trolley line to connect Winter Harbor with Sullivan's Tunk Pond. Winter Harbor historian Allan Smallidge reports Moore's possible intentions to eventually make a circuit drive to Wonsqueak and beyond, much like the park road today. Surrounded as he was by so much journalism, gossip and mythology, Moore and his intentions for development at Schoodic will never be known without more extensive biographical sources. A friend and eulogist noted in print the existence of "extensive improvements which he had in view." How seriously Moore meant to build a "camp" at the summit is an open question. Certainly before his purchases at Schoodic there was ample precedent in Eastern Maine for capping mountaintops with recreational structures. Both Mount Desert's Green Mountain, now Cadillac, and Camden's Mount Battie had early roads or railways to a summit house for tourists, both removed by the early 1900s by more preservation-minded purchasers. It is perhaps hard for visitors now to imagine what Schoodic Head Mountain might be with the framework of a large building looming at the parking lot near the top of what today is quite rugged, primitive-looking (if well-trod) summit terrain.

In any case, John Moore's most obvious legacy for Schoodic is the land he assembled for recreational preservation in the outer Point section, an acquisition of over two thousand acres that created the core of the land area for the modern Schoodic Section of Acadia National Park. But Moore's ambitions were frozen in time, for he died abruptly just short of age fifty-two, seemingly of a heart attack in June 1899, before any other improvement could be launched. Hence Acadia National Park's land might have been rescued from further development—this time from the ambitions and vision of the man known today as its savior and preserver.

CHAPTER 10

AFTER A GENERATION IN LIMBO, A NATIONAL PARK

A turning point in Schoodic's preservation was its fateful good fortune to lie in limbo for a whole generation, from 1899 to the early 1930s. This fortuitous transition occurred because for twenty-eight years, despite their diminishing interest in the community, Moore's widow and daughters

The Grindstone Neck cottage of Moore's daughter, Faith, who played a key role in preserving Schoodic for a generation and helping Dorr secure it as a national park.

continued honoring his wishes or ambitions by holding the land that makes up the park—even rounding out its original holdings in Lower Harbor a few months after Moore's death. They did this despite the discouragement of land taxes doubling over the course of two decades for Schoodic Point and even after his widow, Louise, and daughter Ruth had moved to England and sold most of their family holdings in the nearby Grindstone colony. That colony's revived improvement company also took over the heirs' interest in the 3,400-acre wooded Birch Harbor Mountain territory, the green band of Schoodic Woods that Moore had bought east and north of the original park. But fortunately for the future park, Moore's unmarried daughter, Faith, retained a picturesque cottage and substantial property in the Grindstone neighborhood along with a commitment to the area. Though she lived much in England, she seems to have taken the lead in sustaining the heirs' interest in preserving her father's first Schoodic purchases for use by the Grindstone colonists as well as the local community.[48]

THE LONG HIATUS

During this long hiatus from development, Schoodic Point went through a substantial change. As it passed from being recently uninhabited and "unused" to being an abandoned development venture, this vast area assumed the character of a large vacant lot. Like any vacant lot, it was an area in transition with potential for public abuse or for conversion to a new future. Now for the first time, the Point gradually became an open terrain for general public access, and oral reports indicate that a variety of people were regularly passing through this almost deserted region.

For a generation, John Moore's carriage roads slowly deteriorated but remained in use. The passageway that is now the Alder Path and had been Moore's carriage road down to Blueberry Hill and "the ponds" had become a rough track navigable by a Model T with trailer to launch small boats at East Pond. Yet much of the land around Frazer Point and along the carriage road on the shore as far as Raven's Nest remained open land with few trees, as shown in photos from the early 1930s. Grindstone colonists and the local public frequented this land for boating, hunting, recreation and use in fishing camps at East Pond. A hunting camp was maintained at Frazer Point and another at Pond Island, formerly Welch's

This log causeway from the mainland over the marsh to Big Moose "Island" was the only land access to the end of Schoodic Point before 1932. *Courtesy of National Park Service, Acadia National Park, Motor Road Construction Reports.*

Island, on West Pond, while trails with a log walkway were made over the marsh to Big Moose. At Arey Cove on Little Moose Island, six Coombs brothers kept a family summer base camp and fish house to be near their traps and nets. Old logging roads became trails and carriage paths over the heights of Schoodic Head and Birch Harbor Mountains, surviving as links between villages to reach friends and relatives or for rusticators to view "the ponds" and visit a local hostelry at Wonsqueak. Local residents skated on the small pond that still survives behind the seawall at Bucks cove. In this era, the rusticators who visited East Pond and gazed toward the end of Schoodic Point may have labeled landmarks in that area with romantic names that were previously unrecorded. The "Anvil" (sometimes "Devil's Anvil") and "Blueberry Hill" (the height at East Pond) are names that later became standard in the park era.[49]

On land that remained relatively open-ledge terrain, the old sheep pastures might have continued in the same grazing use as on the adjoining peninsula at Wonsqueak until the World War I era. During the same period, Crane and Norris houses were mostly unoccupied at Lower Harbor, but Obed Bickford's clan continued in residence nearby with three of his sons' families, where they continued to request a part-time neighborhood school until about 1910.

Last Permanent Residents and New Uncertainties

The new town of Winter Harbor continued to supply local schooling for the Bickford children into the early 1900s, but the patriarch's death in 1917 dispersed the last of the early residents of Lower Harbor. In 1924, too late to benefit the ghost community, two men from nearby harbors, Wilson "Wid" Sargent and Elisha Bridges, finally built a lobster pound and seined herring on Lower Harbor's "Little Point" at the former Myrick-Bickford house site. The Point's last gasp of commercial development came in the 1930s, when an investor, George Harmon, bought Mark Island Lighthouse and then the pound just before it became incorporated within the new national park. He tore down the old Myrick-Bickford house and barn on the small point by the causeway and park entrance, built a new pound keeper's residence and staffed it with the family of manager George Delaney until the World War II draft cleared out these last residents at Lower Harbor.

As Lower Harbor's villagers gradually evaporated in the early 1900s, its sister village to the east at Wonsqueak and Bunkers Harbors was experiencing a renaissance. This was partly due to the excellent harbor facility at Bunkers that served the burgeoning lobster fishery. But growth

Harmon's Lower Harbor lobster pound (1926–40s) was managed by George Delaney (light trousers). *Collection of Katherine Delaney Ross.*

here was accelerated by the construction of two pioneering lobster pounds, the first in the region, built by Ezra Over and Frank Huckins at Bunkers in 1896. With these facilities at the core of a growing fishery, more and more lobster boats called these harbors their homeport; even the narrow Wonsqueak Harbor moorings held a dozen boats by the 1940s. The contrast between these two fishing outposts of the Schoodic Point region is intriguing, starting as they did in the 1800s at almost equal populations and ending with Lower Harbor as the park's ghost village.

THE ROAD TO BECOMING A NATIONAL PARK

During the years after World War I, the effect of land taxes began to play a major part in decisions about development or preservation at Schoodic. Moore's widow had remarried, and his daughter Ruth had moved on, marrying the British Viscount Lee and settling with her sister Faith in the English countryside to pursue interests far removed from Schoodic. But the gradually increasing taxes on their Schoodic land were to double over two decades—even in the somewhat sheltered town of Winter Harbor, which John Moore's associates had helped create in part to modify the weight of land taxes. In time, taxes would have to become a growing concern for Moore's heirs and, more than likely, an underlying issue at George Dorr's fortuitous meeting at a Jordan Pond House dinner in September 1922 with Moore's widow, Louise Leeds, at which they discussed the status of Schoodic Point.

The model for Acadia National Park's land preserve as a public benefit was a Massachusetts trusteeship started in 1892 by Harvard president Charles Eliot's son, a frequent rusticator at Mount Desert. After 1901, George Dorr and Eliot Sr. applied this concept to watershed conservation and mountaintop lands on Mount Desert, growing a land preservation movement on Mount Desert Island, the Hancock County Trustees of Reservations. As the trusteeship gained considerable momentum and more land, tax-free status for the land became a major motivation. In 1913, Eliot and Dorr were forced by punitive Maine tax politics to seek national monument status (and soon national park status) as a way to protect Mount Desert's mountaintops from state tax liability. Dorr's persuasiveness and connections brilliantly sold the preservation concept first to President Wilson as a national monument and then to Congress in 1918–19 as Lafayette National Park. The name, honoring our revolutionary French freedom fighter and World War I ally, was chosen to help promote support "because of the strong war-time feeling at the time," said Dorr.[50]

Schoodic as a Park Prospect

Dorr was still actively using the Trustees of Public Reservations as a private vehicle for acquiring and transferring new land for the park area on Mount Desert when, in 1922, he had a seemingly chance dinner meeting with Moore's widow, Louise Leeds. He registered agreeable surprise as she "asked if I would not like to have her interest, a third, in Schoodic Peninsula." The next day, the two led a party up the still-navigable old horse road to the summit of Schoodic Head Mountain and from there resolved to persuade Moore's heirs in England to join in the gift. Long and complex situations intervened, including the death of Louise and the threat that the Schoodic land would have to be bought on behalf of an adoptive heir, before Dorr, with "no slight amount of tactful handling," was able to secure the gift to the trustees in 1927. The heirs' main explicit requirement was to open it for "the public and in memory of the late John G Moore." But Dorr realized that there was still one important condition from the Moore donors, Louise's heirs and Faith and Ruth Lee, now "Lady Lee," in England. As avid Anglophiles, they had always been unwilling to donate Schoodic for inclusion in such a French-named entity as "Lafayette Park." Dorr, realizing he would need a different name to save his Schoodic negotiation, as well as the newly expanded park, announced that he had often thought the name "Acadia, because of its old historical associations and descriptive character, would have been far better." So, with Dorr's successful lobbying for a bigger national park, the name "Acadia" was created, which unwittingly would soon launch thousands of new businesses in Hancock County. Dorr's "tactful handling" with the Moore heirs likely included reminders of the tax costs of Schoodic land, which in 1926 had just abruptly increased by nearly another 50 percent. In any case, by 1929, his trusteeship had deftly arranged for over two thousand acres of outer Schoodic Point and some other areas to become part of a newly expanded and renamed Acadia National Park. At last, the Point had become a preserved park open to the general public.

Visitors at Schoodic today might not easily recognize the terrain that was the park of 1929. The road off the height north of Frazer Creek down to

George B. Dorr, founder of the park first as a land trust, then as Lafayette National Park and finally as Acadia National Park with the addition of Schoodic in 1929. *Courtesy of National Park Service, Acadia National Park.*

Moore's stone-and-wood bridge (the bridgehead still visible) was an abrupt drop, and the main access on the old horse roads to the mountain and the overlook on East Pond, now Blueberry Hill, were badly overgrown and degraded. There was no road leading beyond the extensive tidal marsh standing between the mainland and a completely deserted Big Moose Island, nor was there a clear path there or to the famous crashing surf at the end of the Point. No park ranger was on regular assignment at Schoodic; there was no passage of any kind eastward toward Wonsqueak Harbor and no picnic ground or toilet at the abandoned Lower Harbor village on Frazer Point. In many ways, the whole area continued as it had been since 1899 and during the hiatus period, with little visible evidence of park status.

Perhaps George Dorr, as Acadia National Park director, would have been content to see outer Schoodic Point continue forever in this original primitive condition. His view on the park's land, as later reported by the Rockefellers, favored "leaving it wild" for the quiet pursuit of nature in an undeveloped state, accessible to the "woods wise" hiker and appreciative naturalist. Such views were accused by some of being rather elitist—a term more negative now than it was in 1929. As the Depression came on, such a term would gain negative momentum, but Dorr was above all a political realist and quite ready to adapt to changing conditions.[51]

CHAPTER 11

SCHOODIC'S THIRD PHASE OF DEVELOPMENT

Schoodic by 1930 had become part of America's national treasure—its preserved national parks. While Dorr, as director of Acadia National Park, had not yet launched any improvements for the new section at the Point, some road improvements were considered and a station built in 1931 to give a base for a possible part-time ranger near John Moore's mountain road off West Pond. On Mount Desert Island, however, more ambitious plans were underway for park development, spurred by the enormously wealthy John D. Rockefeller Jr., the third tycoon to oversee the next phase of development at Schoodic.

Rockefeller's devotion to public philanthropy since the World War I era was much focused on Mount Desert Island, where he had settled in a Tudor-beamed "cottage" in 1910. Energized by his vision that preserved land should be seen by an appreciative public and made accessible to visitors, and with a disposition toward carefully planned engineering, Rockefeller quietly and steadily bought land adjacent to the emerging Acadia National Park. By 1930, he had already overcome objections by some rusticators to building carriage roads on preserved land and had tenaciously completed an aggressive program of personally supervised horse carriage road and bridge construction, mostly on his land but also partly on areas owned by the park or the trustees. Most of these cooperative arrangements he accomplished by carrot-and-stick negotiations with Dorr and the park administrators, with his future land donations always on the horizon. The next step in Rockefeller's vision for the '30s was to extend his program for access by motor roads,

A shore section of Moore's carriage roadbed as used by the park's road builders, 1932. *Courtesy of National Park Service, Acadia National Park, Motor Road Construction Reports.*

already completed and donated for Jordan and Bubble Ponds. He was now ready to fund and oversee construction of a summit motor route over parkland to Cadillac Mountain but was especially keen to build the Ocean Drive (today's Park Loop motor road around Otter Cliffs) principally on land he owned and would soon donate. Before long, his vision would have a direct impact on the landscape at Schoodic.

George Dorr was enlisted by Rockefeller to help him deal with an inconvenient obstruction to his Ocean Drive plan: a highly successful World War I–era international radio signal station that stood immediately in his path, owned by the U.S. Navy near the heights of Otter Cliffs. Rockefeller was eager to persuade the Navy to situate the station elsewhere but must have been pleased to see George Dorr claiming credit for identifying Schoodic Point, during the spring and summer of 1930, as the only available mainland alternative to Otter Cliffs. Rockefeller is said to have promptly helped further this idea by hiring a physicist to test and verify good radio reception at Schoodic.[52]

A Plutocrat's Focus on Schoodic

Apparently, both Dorr and Rockefeller were willing to compromise the newly preserved status of Schoodic in favor of their vision of public progress. In Dorr's words, "No site less favorable [than Otter Cliffs] would be acceptable, in exchange, to the Navy Department, I knew, and there was but one location which I thought might equal it—the far seaward projection of Schoodic Peninsula, the Park's recent acquisition." In fact, Rockefeller was also directly involved in promoting the Schoodic alternative and personally surveyed the site at Big Moose in mid-May 1930. By now, Rockefeller's golden finger was directed at Schoodic Point, and Dorr promptly sought Navy brass to look favorably on this mainland location, soon securing the consent of "the Secretary of the Navy himself...an old friend of mine in Boston." Then, with Rockefeller pushing for a deadline, Dorr strove to overcome the Navy's technical objections and find federal funding. With the help of David Rodick, as attorney for the Trustees of Public Reservations, Dorr brought critical Navy radio experts on the scene and secured an encouraging report: "There could be no question, they said, as to the exceptional radio receptive fitness of the Schoodic site. Objection could center only on the relative isolation for its personnel." Eventually, after pushing engineers to confirm water and power capabilities, Dorr helped pull enough strings in Washington to confirm a deal by 1932. Congress would fund the buildings for the new station and, with help from the park budget, a road to reach it. Rockefeller was, of course, pleased to open the way for his Ocean Drive, whose construction he oversaw in 1933 while keeping close watch on work done on the new road at Schoodic. Here he took an active interest in road construction and in promoting the entire process of park development wherever it needed help, as in funding the drilling of artesian wells to supply the new base. It seems likely that he and Dorr, through trusteeship associates, were behind the 1933 purchase and park donation of the core twenty-six-acre plot for the radio station and probably also the remaining abandoned lots at Lower Harbor, including two on the north bank. In a final grand philanthropic gesture, Rockefeller signaled his pleasure in this newly accessible Schoodic District of the park by furnishing the design and engineering for six buildings at the new base, including funding for an elegant new brick-and-beam "Acadian lodge" building designed by his architect Grosvenor Atterbury. He hoped thereby to set a park-like tone for the new Navy radio signal base that would open in early 1935. In time, Atterbury's new structure became known as the "Rockefeller Building."

THE ROAD TO THE RADIO STATION
CREATES A NEW SCHOODIC

All the machinations for Schoodic among these patricians did not occur in a social or political vacuum, of course. With the Navy involved, the federal government was now committed to an interest in the outer Point. When Depression-era politics produced a New Deal job-corps program, the Civilian Conservation Corps (CCC), Schoodic became a model target for parkland improvement, as well as for a modern military installation. To overcome the "relative isolation" of Big Moose, the Navy project would require a new four-mile road and infrastructure work on a large scale, including buildings, utilities and facilities for the radio station. To those who for a generation had grown up familiar with the nearly abandoned and undisturbed Schoodic terrain, such massive federal intervention must have seemed like a space-era rocket ship landing upon the moon. Federally managed crews set to work in 1933–34 to build a new causeway bridge, demolish the old Lower Harbor buildings to create a cleared area at Frazer Point, build the long roadway to the base and solidify the old Moore mountain road. The new motor road of 1933 followed most of Moore's tracks of 1897–98. An interesting part of the project was a CCC brush- and wood-clearing operation, removing deadwood and drastically thinning alder, spruce, birch, jack pine and maple to open views from the new roadway, while choosing to spare fir, poplar and tamarack trees, as well as rhodora and viburnum shrubs. Along the way, they amassed 230 cords of firewood along a new power path to the base. The roadbed, finished with a pink-granite asphalt-gravel surface, grew from a new causeway bridge at Frazer Creek, along the west shore of the Point, overland to West Pond and up to the new ranger cabin facility near Moore's mountain road. But the new road went farther, across a new causeway past West Pond, along its marshland and on to the radio station entrance on the east side of Big Moose. Then, in 1934–35, it extended to a new and artfully sited motor traffic parking area for viewing the now-famous spectacular surf on the end of Schoodic Point. A construction project of this scale involved much heavy trucking and steam-driven road and rock-drilling equipment to make dozens of substantial ledge cuts, all needing large numbers of grateful local men to be mobilized into the workforce.

At the end of this train of construction loomed the new twenty-six-acre Navy radio base, with two two-hundred-foot antenna and six new buildings, including Rockefeller's Acadian brick-and-beam contribution. Anticipating

Jackhammer roadwork on the ledge at West Pond, once a landing site for logging operations in the 1830s and '40s. *Courtesy of National Park Service, Acadia National Park, Motor Road Construction Reports.*

The tide at West Pond once flowed through the gap in the foreground but is now mostly blocked by today's road and causeway connecting us to Big Moose "Island" and SERC.

the base's scheduled opening at the beginning of 1935, the National Park Service in 1934 was able to buy (from the GLIC successors) a two-hundred-foot wide swath of shoreland along Wonsqueak Bay and Harbor. In the spring of 1935, a contractor commenced building a Loop Road from the outer Point to Wonsqueak and Bunkers Harbor, reshaping public roads there to improve traffic flow. On its completion, a whole new landscape was in place at outer Schoodic Point, resembling what today's visitor sees. As the new road blasted through ledges, its causeways sealed off several salt ponds and both ends of the salt marshland that once isolated Big Moose "Island" from the mountain and Anvil areas, changing the tidal flow and encouraging forest growth where salt-pan hay had grown. Some photos from this period (see Chapter 10) give us a sense of how the salt marshland appeared before the road changed it.[53]

FURTHERMORE: MOORE'S LEGACY AND THE IDEA OF A PUBLIC PRESERVE

Thirty years after John G. Moore bought and developed the outer section of Schoodic Point as a nature preserve, his land was turned over to George Dorr's Hancock County Trustees of Public Reservations, destined for inclusion in Acadia National Park. His heirs' deed of gift in January 1927 specified the land to be given to the trustees "for use in perpetuo by the public and in memory of the late John G. Moore, former owner." Their deed required that the land be kept "forever as a free public park or for other public purposes and for such other uses as are incidental to the same, including the promotion of biological and other scientific research." Clearly they wanted this gift to be a memorial to Moore, perhaps to be named for him, and available to a broader public and scientific use than Moore himself would have imagined. Little did they suspect that the park's further opening "for other public purposes" would involve the construction of a U.S. Navy base in its midst. The building of the base and its roadways was a consuming preoccupation; it took another ten years after his heirs' gift before Moore's role in the new park would finally be memorialized. In 1937, his name was given to the highway from Winter Harbor leading to the park, and a bronze plaque honoring his contribution was placed at the parking lot overlooking the dramatic surf at the end of the Point.

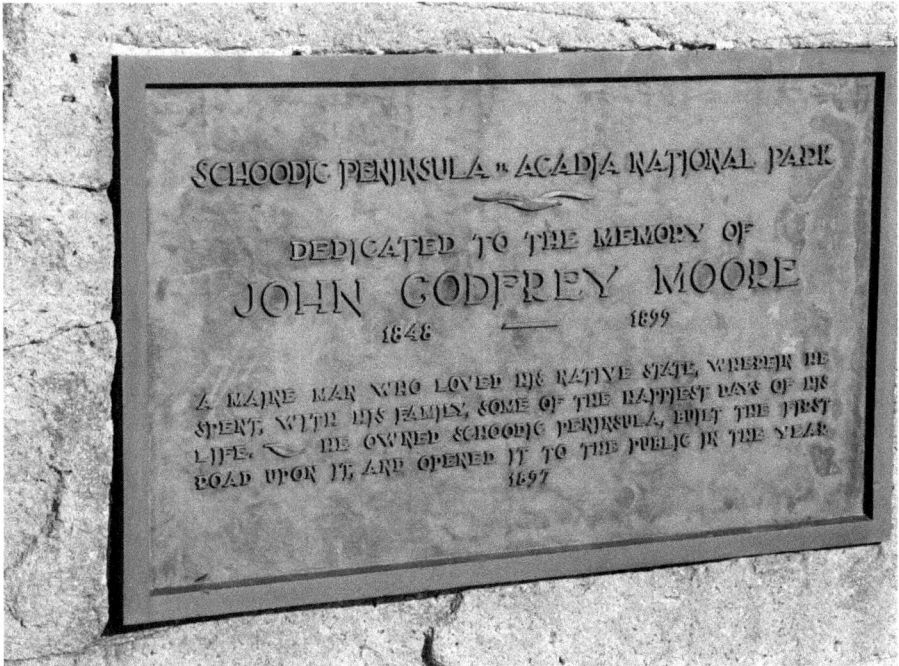

This bronze plaque honoring John G. Moore is located in the parking lot at the end of Schoodic Point.

After the passage of that much time, the memorial plaque was framed to credit Moore (incorrectly) with a "first road" into the park area and with an intention to open the land freely to the public. But on the showing of Moore's career, his carriage roads and his plans for stables and hunting lodges, his land was meant to remain private, and his idea of "the public" seemed to mean principally the rusticators, the people he would invite from the Grindstone colony and their friends (see Chapter 9). In this, Moore was undoubtedly a product of his times and his social milieu. His idea of a public benefit would resemble that of Charles Eliot, who viewed all of the inhabited property on Mount Desert Island as a preserve that should be "treated as a park" for "the summer residents trying to preserve the natural beauties." During the mid-1890s, it is unlikely that Moore could have easily found an appropriate model for a state or national nature preserve that was open to the general public in the East, even if he had an inclination to create one. Although the late 1800s had seen the creation of Yellowstone and state preserves at Yosemite and the Adirondacks, "in each case wilderness preservation was almost accidental and certainly not the result of a national movement," as Roderick Nash observed about the public nature preserves of this era. Theodore Roosevelt, the great advocate and creator of national parks in the early 1900s, had only recently formulated the idea of unspoiled nature preserves as necessary for promoting the nation's need for "a life of strenuous endeavor." Even wilderness pioneer John Muir, the eventual champion of undisturbed and publicly accessible nature preserves, was still in 1897 arguing that selective logging in wilderness parks was as valid a conservation goal as restorative public recreation. In such a setting, Moore's concept of a recreational park to use for anything beyond his own private pleasure would have been relatively advanced for his time. In any case, since Schoodic Point had been so recently inhabited and so extensively logged by local people, Moore would not have seen the region as anything resembling an unspoiled wilderness; if anything, he would see private ownership and restricted access as a conservation measure. Indeed, his nature preserve did not seem to include his ownership of the huge adjacent Schoodic Woods acreage, which had been continuously logged before and after his death.[54]

By 1937, when the Moore plaque was made, our national sense of common facilities open to the general public had already evolved from low-impact use by small populations to a more intensive and motorized access, and if anything, this has grown more intense in the twenty-first century. That change makes it more difficult for us to visualize or appreciate what Moore and his heirs actually hoped for in public land preservation.

CHAPTER 12

A U.S. NAVY BASE AND A DEVELOPED PARK AT SCHOODIC

By the summer of 1935, the outer Point of Schoodic had been completely transformed. What had been a landscape of cut-over forests, abandoned pastures and a ghost village was now a newly minted district of Acadia National Park, with full access provided to the general public by a two-way loop road culminating in the parking lot for viewing spectacular surf at the land's end. Near that was the gateway to the new U.S. Navy base and radio station that would loom even larger than the park in the region's economic environment. Together they evolved in an unusual symbiosis that created the Schoodic Point landscape that appears in the twenty-first century.

THE NAVY BASE: 1935–2002

On Big Moose, no longer really an "island," the U.S. Navy base soon occupied more and more space as its role grew with increasingly sophisticated technology during World War II and the Cold War that followed. It eventually housed the largest residential population that the outer Schoodic Point would ever support. Starting with 26 acres, eleven Navy men and two two-hundred-foot radio towers in 1935, the base soon featured a small forest of ninety-foot towers and antennae supported by heavy guy wires

Grosvenor Atterbury's "Rockefeller Building" was base headquarters in the heyday of the U.S. Navy at Schoodic. It was heavily renovated in 2013.

whose concrete bases remain visible today throughout the forests beyond the buildings. Water was supplied from a well on the base, sewerage was piped into the nearby cove and electricity was carried in on a power line extending south from Winter Harbor through the park to the base. By 1946, the original base had expanded another 156 acres on Big Moose, while a new artesian water supply from the west side of Schoodic Head Mountain was piped southward into the enlarged base. Navy men were living together in a large administrative building (Building 10) until 1951, when ten half-cylindrical metal Quonset huts were erected, housing most of the enlisted men in somewhat primitive conditions until a two-story barracks was built for a growing crew in the 1960s.

In June 1970, the Schoodic Park loop road was changed from a two-way route to one-way traffic from west to east. By one account, the Navy commander requested this to simplify the homecoming route for sailors returning to the base after a night's local revelry, in the process helping local businesses benefit from traffic emerging on the eastern end of the route.

With the demands of the Cold War in the late 1950s through the '70s, the U.S. Navy's operations here became more specialized as a signals intelligence and cryptology center. Worldwide signals were picked up from across Prospect Bay in Corea by a huge circular antenna familiarly dubbed the "elephant cage" but officially called a Circularly Disposed Antenna Array (CDAA) serviced by an operations facility, Building 85. By the 1970s, the operation there expanded, with electromagnetic signals being processed and decoded in a specialized new building, Building 153. All Navy operations connected with the base required high security clearances; the slightest irregularity in a sailor's background was enough to lose security clearance and force his reassignment elsewhere.

The census of 1970 showed that 774 U.S. Navy personnel were permanently stationed here or in nearby Navy housing in Winter Harbor, while large numbers of civilian employees were added to service the facility. The base in the early 1990s supported about 400 Navy men and 300 civilians plus about 300 dependents, substantially enlarging the local Winter Harbor school population. The base area had grown exponentially by leasing parkland around the original core. It eventually featured forty-five buildings for operations, dwelling, cabins, water plants, recreation and storage, all creating a giant military enclave that affected the entire region. Recreational facilities for Navy men included an officer's club and a new ball field built over the site of Jabez Myrick's 1840s farmhouse, reached by a road that, until 2011, was named for the pioneering Myrick family.[55]

Yet this sizeable base, self-contained as it was and supplied with men, food and materials from the outside world, seemed by itself to have little impact on the rest of Schoodic Point's landscape beyond its own fenced-in bounds. Its main environmental effect was probably its road, supply lines and its waste effluent into Arey Cove, which was soon carefully filtered and treated. At its height, the U.S. Navy base benefited the local economy, involving some one thousand military and civilian workers and their dependents and providing numerous military husbands for local ladies. While potentially socially isolating for some as originally feared, the base attracted many servicemen to remain in the region long after their discharge. Its mission, as a largely covert high-security operation, was designed to avoid attracting too much publicity. Tall fences and Navy guards at the gate kept the public away and encouraged park visitors to focus on the undisturbed and remote aspects of Schoodic Point's landscape, most of which consequently managed quite well to evade this gigantic infusion of high technology.

As the century waned, the U.S. Navy base's mission of sensing and decoding worldwide signals over the ocean became obsolete due to the rising technology of satellite sensing equipment. The Navy was forced to scale down its operations on the Point, lay off most of its local employees and eventually close for budgetary reasons. The Schoodic Point base was decommissioned in 2002, its huge facility turned back to the National Park Service, and was soon converted to a new educational center, the Schoodic Education and Research Center (SERC). This renovated campus, through a partnership organization—eventually the Schoodic Institute—was redesigned to house and support biophysical research and science education groups, bringing students and researchers for a different mix of visitor traffic to the Point region.

A DEVELOPED PARK EMERGES

While the Navy base was becoming steadily larger up to the end of the twentieth century, the Schoodic section of Acadia National Park grew at a more modest pace. By 1937, a pier for boat landings had been erected at Frazer Point. Then in the same era came one of the biggest surges of park development: a large infusion of federal money and an increased role for the Civilian Conservation Corps. A CCC temporary base or "side camp" for Schoodic, proposed as early as 1935, was finally set up in 1936–37 with a barracks, kitchen and mess hall located near the new U.S. Navy base. Their work focused on two new projects for the park: a "truck road" from Lower Harbor up into Frazer Cove and thence southward to service the new power path for the base and also a series of hiking trails off Schoodic Head Mountain. These three new trails are the most visible part of the project for today's visitors.

Already in place was the Alder Path, starting from the old ranger cabin area (later a bird research lab) and running southward on John Moore's old carriage road to the Blueberry Hill area. The Schoodic Head trail was built from near the old ranger and bird-research cabin, winding up the west side of the mountain to meet other new trails converging near the upper parking lot of John Moore's mountain road. Here it met another trail started earlier down the east side of the mountain to the Wonsqueak road, the East Trail. It also met a new Anvil Trail constructed down the south side of the mountain,

The Depression-era Civilian Conservation Corps had a base camp on Big Moose in the late 1930s and built many park improvements, including trails. *Courtesy of National Park Service, Acadia National Park, Motor Road Construction Reports.*

The crashing surf on Schoodic Point's ledges is a distinctive attraction for this section of the park. At times, it has proved deceptively dangerous and even lethal.

dropping abruptly to a long ridge southward to climb the Anvil and down to Blueberry Hill. This 1937 CCC trail network, maintained and improved over the years, remained the park's principal trail network into the twenty-first century.[56]

At the end of Schoodic Point, by the surfside parking lot, a bronze plaque was installed in 1937 to commemorate John Moore's conservation of the area in the 1890s—possibly the first general recognition of his early role in preserving this environment. The road to the park from Winter Harbor was named in his honor at the same time, and years later, the park's new auditorium on the SERC campus also bore his name. The surfside parking lot saw further improvements by 1940 with a new CCC-built restroom building, a prototype facility suited to this sparse environment and a forerunner for other embellishments in safety equipment and interpretive signage for this increasingly popular site. In the 1960s, the Frazer Point area also surged in popularity as a picnic ground developed there and became a prime recreational area for Greater Peninsula residents as well as park visitors.

The first regular ranger assigned to the Schoodic District of the park met with a tragic accident in the fall of 1938. Karl Jacobsen, twenty-two, and his young wife were in the woods near the border of the park at Bucks Cove on the Wonsqueak road looking for boundaries and possible signs of pathways when a hunter just outside the park mistook him for deer. He was fatally shot in the stomach by the aged shooter who, devastated, later claimed the wife's hair in the wind had misled him. Yet the ranger, in his last moments, wrote a note to say, "Don't prosecute—not his fault," claiming the cause as his own carelessness. A more fortunate succession of rangers followed him to patrol the park, attempting to avoid the further tragedy of reckless surf-watchers who have on more than one occasion been fatally swept off the rocks, mesmerized by Schoodic's huge storm waves. One of the longest-serving Schoodic rangers, Bill Weidner, has provided watchful security for nearly forty years and witnessed many changes, from the Navy base era to an enlarged park facility.

By century's end, the park had grown in size, with the outer islands, Schoodic and Rolling Islands and some adjacent easements at Wonsqueak added to the preserve. The Schoodic Section of Acadia National Park gradually increased its volume of visitor traffic, thanks to the roadways of 1933–35. A park-related service of "Explorer" buses in 2005 began regular rounds of the loop road and into nearby towns for bicyclists and pedestrians, funded by the Friends of Acadia support group for the national park. According to the park superintendent's estimate, traffic at Schoodic by

2012 had reached 250,000 visitors. Bicycle traffic around the loop expanded exponentially, along with visitor programs at the Education Center, all adding to potential stress on the 1937 trail systems and fragile pathways, as well as newer ones in the Schoodic Woods area. In response, the park's administrators have invested heavily in improved maintenance and remain watchful to contain the inevitable erosion threatened by ever-greater volumes of visitor traffic.

CHANGES AT WONSQUEAK AND BUNKERS HARBORS

With the development of two lobster pounds at Bunkers Harbor in 1896, the harbors here and at Wonsqueak were launched into the mainstream of the twentieth-century lobster fishery. The pounds, sold by the builders to a large Rockland firm in the 1910s, did a growing business subsequently managed for the owners by new families from nearby, and the harbors filled up with small motorized fishing craft.[57] Nearly all the village fishing families identified themselves in the 1920 census specifically as "lobster fisherman," with Bunkers the homeport for all on the eastern shore of the Point region up to Birch Harbor. By the 1940s, even the tiny harbor at Wonsqueak, almost as closed in and tided out as West Pond, supported eight one-man lobster boats, a waterfront herring seine operation and a growing population. No longer a backwater, the region was opened to new local families during the two World War eras and especially by the rebuilding of the highway from the park and Navy in the 1930s. But by century's end, changes in fishing technology and the loss of the herring fishery saw Bunkers crowded with newer and larger lobster boats, fishing craft all but gone from Wonsqueak, the pound itself less used and vacation homes now more visible on the Point region's shoreline.

FURTHERMORE: A SCHOODIC OF THE MIND FOR NOTABLE ARTISTS

The beauty of Schoodic Point seems to resonate on some level with almost every visitor. Since the park opened, probably hundreds of thousands have recorded their reaction to this elemental landscape and seascape using a camera, and many others have used paint. Films have been made, some for advertisements but often in a travelogue format, some with a soundtrack of original music. By selecting, choosing and shaping the way they capture their experience of Schoodic Point, these artful viewers construct their works with the expectations and mental images they bring to the scene or with those to be evoked for an intended audience.

The surf at the end of Big Moose Island is by far the favorite subject for many visitors. The spectacle of massive waves from the open ocean smashing into an exposed rocky shore is likely to excite awe at a terrifying natural power, even an ecstatic feeling that philosophers have called "the sublime." For others, the focus may be on a serene ocean contrasted with sturdy trees or shrubs and granite to call up such sensations as calm, solitude or loneliness, harmony with nature or mystery in shrouded fog. A trained artist, bringing disciplined skills to this scenery, can transform it to create a rich array of responses to the Point for a receptive audience. A few examples from the work of renowned artists in past decades might suggest how the Schoodic scene has evoked a range of complex feelings and given the Point a distinctive presence as a motif in the arts.

The most celebrated artist of black-and-white landscape photography in modern times is undoubtedly Ansel Adams, whose work at Schoodic was published in the late 1940s. A print of *1948 at Schoodic* was included in his anthology *My Camera in the National Parks*. His focus here was entirely on the textures of water and atmosphere off the Point, with emphasis on luminous clouds and the light effects of patterned ocean surface receding to the horizon. A similar interest in the sea was featured in his 1949 print *The Atlantic: Schoodic Point, Acadia National Park*, but here the focus was almost entirely on the flow of seawater over ledges, the horizon barely visible, with a close-up of the streaming wave washing smoothly across the foreground. In neither of these did Adams show any interest in a classic Winslow Homer–like towering wave or smashing surf. During the late '40s and early '50s, the renowned photo artist Bernice Abbott was also active in making images at Schoodic. She has been followed by scores of other great artists, including many whose talents developed in the culture capital of New York.

In the early 1940s, the power of massive surf at the Point was most famously given artistic expression by the painter Marsden Hartley. Working in the Schoodic region at the end of his life, Hartley focused his intense spiritual vision on the monumental effects of immense breaking waves, notably in two paintings in major museums. Though he had done notable

This modernist abstraction, titled *Schoodic*, encapsulates the elements of the Point's features. The artist, Chenoweth Hall (1908–1999), was heavily influenced by watercolorist John Marin. *Courtesy of Miriam Colwell.*

surfscapes in the 1930s, in these late Schoodic works, he was devoted entirely to the towering force of white-foam waves rising above the horizon. One of these, *The Wave* of 1940–41 (Worcester Art Museum), shows two mountainous white cones of water erupting beyond a rampart of granite blocks, clearly the parking lot stones at Schoodic Point. The same dark granite blocks appear in the foreground of a still more elemental work, *Evening Storm, Schoodic Maine* of 1942 (Brooklyn Museum of Art). Featuring a huge wave against a very dark cloud-scattered sky, the work is reminiscent of Albert Ryder, whose somewhat primitive and ghostly work had been an early influence on Hartley. Both paintings, as with many Hartley landscapes, were not based on any sketch made on the scene but were entirely re-created in his imagination in later studio work. Hartley, unable to drive a car and driven to Schoodic by friends, was known to have silently stared at the breaking waves, absorbing their awesome power and not reconstructing his vision until weeks later. Another painter of comparable fame, the water colorist John Marin, did his best-known seascapes elsewhere but painted at Schoodic during his frequent visits, where he also made an interesting drawing, again focused on wave and water action. Here the land is barely visible; the interest is all in making the water come alive with the vibrant dynamics of active wave patterns in the ocean off the Point. A Gouldsboro painter of the Schoodic scene, Chenoweth Hall, was deeply influenced by her association and friendship with Marin.

An interesting example of how Schoodic has served as stimulus for literary work appears in an often-reprinted poem by the late poet Amy Clampitt. Her dense lyric piece "Low Tide at Schoodic" of the early 1980s is a meditation on scenery of the region written while summering in a rental at nearby Corea. In it she uses the immediate experience of slow-rolling waves, low-tide barnacled boulders and yellow warblers in the surrounding spruces to create imagery linked to a mental world of revolution and violence, contrasting with the immediate serene air of calm detachment. The sound of the warbler's song is characterized as "a wiry wheeze" and his neck markings as "a noose of dark," drawing on the writer's lifelong and intense familiarity with birds expressed in several of her other poems. As with the other artists noted here, the Schoodic scene has been an occasion to project intense feelings evoked by the strong elements of the Point's landscape.[58]

CHAPTER 13

PRESERVATION VERSUS DEVELOPMENT IN A NEW CENTURY

B y the end of the twentieth century, the ecology of most of outer Schoodic Point had survived and recovered for well over a century from its earlier logging, farming, pasturage and harbor usage. The Schoodic landscape had accommodated its early developers and settlers in a precarious balance with its sparse conditions. And even as these settlers' lands were abandoned,

The Schoodic Education and Research Center (SERC) and former U.S. Navy base is located on the east side of the outer Point, across from Little Moose Island.

followed by aborted threats of resort development, much of the region's open land managed to remain undisturbed, the outer Point becoming a largely preserved, if somewhat compromised, parkland. Despite the development of a large military base at its core, the land under preservation at the park had quietly grown back to a more well-rounded ecosystem by the end of the twentieth century. Except for the base and roadwork, the outer sections of the Schoodic Point region could almost pass for an undisturbed (if not wild) natural environment.

THE SCHOODIC EDUCATION AND RESEARCH CENTER (SERC)

Possible future uses of the decommissioned U.S. Navy base on Big Moose Island had been deliberated locally for two years before Acadia National Park in 2002 took over the facility to make it the largest of several "education and research centers" run by the National Park Service. The facility therefore became a park entity called the Schoodic Education and Research Center, generally known by its acronym, SERC. Local supporters were optimistic that the former base might play the large economic and employment role that the Navy base had fulfilled; they hoped that a large research-based institution like the Jackson Laboratory on Mount Desert Island could somehow be induced to occupy the old base. To develop possible research programs at the center, and to manage the facility for a role consistent with the rest of Acadia National Park's mission, a private foundation was formed in Winter Harbor to operate as a park concession in partnership with the National Park Service. Initially named Acadia Partners for Research and Learning, the partnership strove to find a "flagship" research-based company or educational institution to operate in the facility, but candidates willing to invest or relocate into this remote location were hard to find. The opening years of the center were devoted to a gradual process of defining a role that stressed the "education" end of the equation, with emphasis on teacher-training facilities and student environmental education workshops. The center also encouraged the arts by hosting an international sculpture symposium that met in alternate years on the campus, delighting the public as it watched sculptors working noisily on granite pieces in front of the Rockefeller Building. Meanwhile, funds furnished by the Navy, by way of

The auditorium at Schoodic Education and Research Center was named in honor of Point conservationist John G. Moore.

an exit grant, enabled a large modern auditorium to be built, providing an attractive new media-rich venue for classroom and public presentations. It was formally dedicated on August 6, 2007, and named for Schoodic's now-famous first preservationist, John G. Moore. In 2010, a federal grant enabled the center over the next year to rebuild the entire base into a new campus to be operated by the partnership, soon renamed the SERC Institute and then Schoodic Institute. Unsustainable buildings were removed and others radically renovated, and trees were extensively cleared for newly landscaped grounds to make a revived campus of dormitory, classroom and science learning laboratory facilities. In the following years, the Acadia National Park presence expanded at the center with staff to provide student programs, teacher training and science education. A program of "artists in residence" was developed with a fellowship for visiting artisans, summer research workshops were promoted for various groups and the old ranger station at the foot of Schoodic Head was renovated for specialized research on local and especially migratory birds. Although the large former base facility was not easy for the park and the partnership to maintain financially, SERC's first decade of redefined activity showed promise in making the old base a new focus of activity with a different set of visitors to appreciate the Schoodic environment.

The Birch Harbor Mountain Schoodic Woods

Still in an uncertain state in the new century was the Schoodic Point region's green band of land to the north, encircling Acadia National Park up to its boundary, the hilly ridge of Birch Harbor Mountain and its extensive Schoodic Woods forest of three thousand-plus acres. This property had been left since Bingham's day as an open area for logging, and except for dwelling lots sold along Highway 186 between Birch and Winter Harbors, the vast area south of this highway has remained largely uninhabited. During the land boom of 1887, the property had been bought from the Bingham proprietorship by Luere Deasy to be combined with lands of speculator Charles Hutchings, soon merged with other properties into a great consortium centered on the emerging Grindstone Neck colony: the Gouldsboro Land Improvement Company. The company's immediate goal was to secure Birch Harbor Pond and its watershed as a source of water for the colony and for what became the new township of Winter Harbor. The pond also served into the 1950s for ice harvesting—a local source for refrigeration in the summer—while the forested areas were subject to considerable logging over the years. The Birch Harbor Mountain ridges, nearly devoid of trees, are visible in the company's 1890s photos promoting the new Grindstone colony. In 1934, the company sold the two-hundred-foot wide strip of shore that enabled Acadia National Park to complete its 1937 loop roadway to Wonsqueak Harbor. But tree cutting proceeded on the land to the north of the park, especially after the company and its successor trust gave up the remaining land to timber purchasers in the 1950s. Three logging efforts along the ridges and slopes of Birch Harbor Mountain were recorded in the last four decades of the century, most recently by a foreign-based capital holding company that owned it. By the 1990s, the view north from Schoodic Head Mountain showed terrain laced with rough roadways and heavy timber cutting.[59]

Opposite, top: The land in view from Schoodic Head to Schoodic Mountain to the north risked development as an "eco-resort" until it was bought for conservation in late 2012.

Opposite, bottom: Schoodic's history is still on view—John G. Moore's road bridgehead can be seen here by the causeway at Frazer Creek.

The foreign-based company that owned the Birch Harbor Mountain Schoodic Woods property began publicizing plans in 2007 to develop a massive recreational "eco-resort" projected to occupy nearly all of its forested green-band area. In a public meeting in May 2008, they presented a "Vision Statement" plan that would fill much of the area with golf links, luxury housing, a large hotel/lodge with marina near the park entrance and a kayaking marina at the eastern park exit, thus framing the entire park with commercial facilities. The plan suggested a "wildlife corridor" that would narrow the two-mile-wide green band of Birch Harbor Mountain forest to a half mile, squeezed between two densely built housing areas and traversed by a residential access road. The plan, surrounding the park and totally engulfing and enclosing the Point's isolated landscape with the trappings of a luxury resort culture, was clearly aimed at exploiting the park for private gain. The initial proposal actually offered to replace the public's automobile access to the park with "eco-friendly" golf cart traffic controlled by the resort.

By the summer of 2008, Acadia National Park administrators, as well as the park's support group, Friends of Acadia, and several environmental groups, were mobilized against the resort project, hoping to organize a mixed-conservation purchase of the Schoodic Woods property as crucial to maintaining the Point region's character. For some years, the foreign-based owners made no response to these efforts for a conservation-oriented purchase, but their development plans slowly went dormant through the severe recession period that followed.[60]

As the economy remained unsettled over the next four years, particularly in the developer-owner's home markets in Europe, recession pressures appear to have motivated them to abandon their "eco-resort" project and sell the entire 3,300-acre property in late 2011. The sale, to a timber company primarily interested in logging and development north of the Schoodic Point region, was arranged with active help from Friends of Acadia and especially from the conservation group Maine Coast Heritage Trust. The terms of their purchase included an option for the trust to purchase a 1,000-acre conservation easement south of Highway 186 in the forest area around the ridges of Birch Harbor Mountain and down to the Acadia National Park boundaries. In 2012–13, a plan was announced to build a 130-acre campground on the west slope of Birch Harbor Mountain, supported by the timber company with an anonymous family foundation and in consultation with the trust, Friends of Acadia and park officials. Construction began in 2014 on a campground site close to the park entrance. The plan included the prospect that Acadia National Park might in time take control of this campground and much of the Birch Mountain terrain, taking on a new network of foot and bicycle trails linked to existing ones.[61]

These outcomes were destined to produce a new pattern of population pressure on the landscape of the Schoodic Point region. The area under preservation was occupied by the early settlers in their heyday with a maximum year-round population of 82 people, but the same land with its added facilities may potentially carry a summer population of far greater numbers. The Schoodic Woods campground, with a minimum feasible number of one hundred sites, was designed to house up to 300 visitors, while the programs and dormitories at SERC had a capacity for 125 overnight guests. This allows a potential 425 people per day living here for six months yearly, in addition to day visitors in the park and at SERC. The growth of these facilities for increased visitor traffic creates a different equation of pressures between nature preservation and recreational development.

Seeking a Balance of Development and Preservation

Such volatile changes in the prospects of the Schoodic Point region in the early twenty-first century could be seen as a compressed version of the tensions the region had earlier experienced more slowly over several centuries. At times, the Point area was neglected and left to grow with little or no human intervention, yet at other intervals, its fragile ecology was subject to intense pressures to produce a direct economic benefit for its owners or to meet a growing demand for recreational experience. Then there are stretches of time when the region seems to achieve a certain balance between these extremes. For Schoodic, this makes a distinctive kind of cyclic tension, a process that will probably continue. The process seems almost rhythmic, echoing the interchange of elemental forces in this apparently timeless landscape, where the visitor expects to feel the clash of seas and granite, watch forest green grappling with arid ledge or sense the contrasts of clear air and fog on either side of the Point.

NOTES

Preamble

1. The "Enrage" name is reported from 1686 French sources by Charles B. McLane and Carol McLane, *Islands of the Mid-Maine Coast, Volume II: Mount Desert to Machias Bay* (Woolwich, ME: Kennebec River Press, 1989), 208. A French map of 1702 identifying the Point as "Pointe Escaudet" is reproduced in Harald E.I. Prins and Bunny McBride, *Asticou's Island Domain: Wabanaki Peoples at Mount Desert Island, 1500–2000*, 2 vols. (Boston: National Park Service, 2007), I: 177. For the Schoodic name derivation, see Fanny Eckstorm, *Indian Place Names of the Penobscot Valley and the Maine Coast* (Orono: University of Maine Press, 1978), 211.
2. Abandoned settlements elsewhere in Acadia National Park are described in Kimberly Sebold, "Lilacs, Cellar Holes, and the Courthouse, " *Maine History* 42, no. 2 (April 2005): 1–20.

Chapter 1

3. The term "Schoodic soil" first appeared in soil survey of Hancock County by USDA geologists, partly to describe an area on Swan's Island. It is

characterized as an ultra-thin, gravelly soil ten inches thick or less, lying on granite slopes at a grade of 5 percent to 15 percent. It is considered unsuitable for cultivation and barely suitable for logging. See H. Almquist and A.J.P. Calhoun, "A Coastal Southern-Outlier Patterned Fen," *Northeast Naturalist* 10, no. 2 (2003): 121.

4. Samuel de Champlain, *Les Voyages du Sieur de Champlain* (Paris: Jean Berjon), 40.

5. The "wall of rocks" quote is from *Bar Harbor Record* 11, no. 55 (November 17, 1897): 4.

Chapter 2

6. The complex and delicately balanced plant ecology of peninsulas in the Schoodic region is described in Bruce T. Milne and Richard T.T. Forman, "Peninsulas in Maine: Woody Plant Diversity, Distance, and Environmental Patterns," *Ecology* 67, no. 4 (1986): 967–74.

7. William B. Krohn and Christopher Hoving, *Early Maine Wildlife* (Orono: University of Maine Press, 2010), 1–45.

8. John P. Mosher, "Report on Faunal Remains from the Frazer Point Site ME 487-008," Maine Historic Preservation Commission, 2002.

9. Bunny McBride and Harald E.L. Prins, *Indians in Eden: Wabanakis and Rusticators on Maine's Mount Desert Island, 1840s–1920s* (Camden, ME: Down East, 2009), 81.

10. Molly Schauffler and George Jacobsen Jr., "Persistence of Coastal Spruce Refugia During the Holocene in Northern New England, USA, Detected by Stand-Scale Pollen Stratigraphies," *Journal of Ecology* 90 (2002): 244. See also Molly Schauffler, "Paleoecology of Coastal and Interior Picea or Spruce Stands in Maine," PhD dissertation, University of Maine, 1998.

11. Kristin Hoffman, "Farms to Forests in Blue Hill Bay: Long Island, Maine, as a Case Study in Reforestation," *Maine History* 44, no. 1 (October 2008): 50–76. See also L.E. Conkey, M. Kiefer and A.H. Lloyd, "Disjunct Jack Pine Structure and Dynamics, Acadia National Park, Maine," *Ecoscience* 2 (1995): 169–76; Caitlin McDonough and Chris Arflack, "Acadia's Changing Landscape: Plants and the People That Love Them," slide lecture at Schoodic Education and Research Center, July 20, 2011; and Tom Wessels, *Reading the Forested Landscape: A Natural History of New England* (New York: Countryman Press, 1997).

12. Nonnative species found at these locations included multiflora rose (*Rosa multiflora*), asiatic or oriental bittersweet (*Celastrus orbiculatus*) and bush honeysuckle (*Diervilla lonicera*), as reported by the kindness of botanists Jill Weber, Glen Mittelhauser and Kate Miller (personal communications, April 2, 2013).

Chapter 3

13. The history of native peoples in the Schoodic area is extensively described in Prins and McBride, *Asticou's Island Domain*, I: 55–56, 177–79. Schoodic archaeology reported in Barbara A. Johnson and David Sanger, "Final Report: Archaeological Studies, Investigations, and Excavations at Various Locations, Acadia National Park, Maine," prepared by the University of Maine's Department of Anthropology for the National Park Service, Denver Service Center, 1977. See also David Sanger, "Archeological Investigations at Frazer Point and Duck Harbor, Acadia National Park, Maine," prepared by the University of Maine's Department of Anthropology for the National Park Service, North Atlantic Region, 1981. Also discussed in a talk by Rebecca Cole-Will at SERC, winter 2011.

14. William Cronon, *Changes in the Land: Indians, Colonists, and the Ecology of New England* (New York: Hill and Wang, 1983). Also Eckstorm, *Indian Place Names*, 211, and James Francis, Penebscot tribal historian, lecture at Gouldsboro Historical Society, August 9, 2009.

15. John Livingstone, "A Journal of ye Travails of Major John Livingstone from Annapolis Royall in Nova Scotia to Quebeck in Canada, from Thence to Albany and soe to Boston, October 15 1710 to February 23 1711," *CSP Colonial Series* 25 (1924): 371. Quoted in Prins and McBride, *Asticou's Island Domain*, I: 198.

16. See a 1763 colonial map reproduced in *Historical Researches of Gouldsboro Maine* (Gouldsboro, ME: Gouldsboro, Maine Daughters of Liberty, 1904), frontispiece.

17. John C. Huden, *Indian Place Names of New England* (New York: Museum of the American Indian, 1962), 323.

18. Jonas Crane, "If It's Ghosts You Want at Halloween, Wonsqueak Is the Spookiest," *Bangor Daily News*, October 27, 1963, 6.

Chapter 4

19. Early settlements shown on the *Atlantic Neptune* chart of 1774 for Gouldsboro; settlers' farmsteads are indicated at the heads of bays, and virtually no habitation shows on southern peninsulas, including Schoodic.

20. For background on the Revolutionary and postwar periods, see James Leamon, *The Revolution Downeast: The War for American Independence in Maine* (Amherst: University of Massachusetts Press, 1993). See also Alan Taylor, *Liberty Men and Great Proprietors: The Revolutionary Settlement on the Maine Frontier, 1780–1820* (Chapel Hill: University of North Carolina Press, 1990).

21. For Frazer property records, see Hancock County Deeds (hereafter HCD) 1:405, 6:487, 15:454 and 16:277. This assumes the likelihood that only one Thomas Frazer was living in the Frenchman Bay area at this time. See also Thomas Foss, *A Brief Account of the Early Settlements Along the Shores of Skillings River* (Hancock, ME: 1870), 5, 89.

22. Bingham's lot allocations as surveyed by Samuel Coolidge in 1798 are found in HCD 1:224. For information on Bingham, see Frederick S. Allis Jr., "William Bingham's Maine Lands: 1790–1820," *Colonial Society of Massachusetts* 36 and 37 (1954).

23. For information on the rising fishery, see Wayne O'Leary, *Maine Sea Fisheries: The Rise and Fall of a Native Industry, 1830–1890* (Boston: Northeastern University Press, 1998), 5–39. Road building and whaling activity is recorded in *Gouldsboro Town Records, 1766–1895* (Marco Island, FL: Picton Press, n.d.).

24. For Frisbee's purchases, see HCD 69:502 and 75:402. For information on his roads, see entries for April 1838 and February 1841 in *Gouldsboro Town Records*. For family records, see Allan Smallidge, *Musquito Harbor: A Narrative History* (Winter Harbor, ME: Ironbound Press, 2006), 47. See also Muriel Sampson Johnson, *Early Families of Gouldsboro, Maine* (Marco Island, FL: Picton Press, 1990), 124. Residents in this region are recorded in the U.S. census of 1840 for Gouldsboro. Useful records of local ship ownership, as transcribed from U.S. National Archives shipping records, are presented in Nathalie W. Hahn, *A History of Winter Harbor, Maine* (N.p.: privately published, 1974), 22, 80.

25. For land purchases and logging, see HCD 61:2; 68:249; 79:354; 82:520; 83:375; 87:454, 486–87; 102:419; 104:220; and 106:138. Early cleared areas identified via conversation with the late Casper Sargent (1914–2012) of Winter Harbor.

26. Rockland area limekilns conditions are described in Roger L. Grindle, *Quarry and Kiln: The Story of Maine's Lime Industry* (Rockland, ME: Courier-Gazette, 1971), 4, 7–8.

27. For land purchases and logging, see HCD 61:2; 68:249; 79:354; 82:520; 83:375; 87:454, 486–87; 102:419; 104:220; and 106:138. Early cleared areas identified via conversation with the late Casper Sargent (1914–2012) of Winter Harbor.

Chapter 5

28. The mid-century agriculture for this region is described in Clarence A. Day, *Farming in Maine, 1860–1910* (Orono: University of Maine Press, 1963), 273. For farm tax records of 1890, see Gouldsboro town taxes (located in the town office, Gouldsboro, Maine). For subsistence farming estimates, see Bettye Hobbs Pruitt, "Self-Sufficiency and the Agricultural Economy of Eighteenth-Century Massachusetts," *William and Mary Quarterly* 3, no. 3 (July 1984): 333–63 and Carolyn Merchant, *Ecological Revolutions* (Chapel Hill: University of North Carolina Press, 1989), 180, 278. Gouldsboro's overall farm holdings per capita for 1820 appear to be only slightly higher than these early subsistence estimates, as described by Moses Greenleaf in *A Survey of the State of Maine* (Portland, ME, 1829).

29. The layout of "old Schoodic road" is described in the March 5, 1855 entry in *Gouldsboro Town Records*, 842.

30. Pendleton's journal from 1852 to the mid-1870s was transcribed by Pauline Pendleton Guerrette and her daughter Philippa A. Harvey, who attested to the doctor's habitual travel by one-horse buggy. Transcripts are in the keeping of the Winter Harbor Historical Society. Some typical entries involving produce from these farms and for Arey's transactions include June 7,1852; July 22 and September 26, 1855; November 8, 1858; May 7, 1859; and November 7, 1860.

31. Locations and names of family homesteads for 1860 are shown on "Topographical Map of Hancock County, Maine" (Lee and Marsh), which can be found in the historical societies of Winter Harbor and Gouldsboro. Locations and names of family homesteads and other features for 1881 are shown in *Colby's Atlas of Hancock County*. Family landholdings and relationships appear in HCD 31:467; 69:502; 81:133;

82:516, 520; 83:375; 94:79; 104:395; 108:249; 113:455; 117:488; 120:545–47; 126:164; 127:347; and 136:288.

32. For information on Vinalhaven families, see the 1840 and 1850 U.S. census records for Vinalhaven. For information on Arey family relationships, see Donald Arey, *Genealogy of the Arey Family* (Self-published, 1984). For Norris and Holmes families, see Johnson, *Early Families*, 141, 197–98. Myrick's fish schooner ownership is recorded in Hahn, *History of Winter Harbor*, 87.

Chapter 6

33. For typical sea fishery patterns through the Civil War era, see O'Leary, *Maine Sea Fisheries*, 20–95. Ship and crew records for this neighborhood are transcribed in Hahn, *History of Winter Harbor*, 86–87. Joy's ownership is recorded in the Hancock County Probate Registry, Docket 2728. For fish-making and salt costs, see O'Leary, *Maine Sea Fisheries*, 145–50; for marketing, see 36–39, 136.

34. In U.S. census records for Gouldsboro for 1850 and 1860–70, the town's households and dwellings are listed in a sequence that follows land ownership patterns that establish neighborhood clusters and household arrangements.

35. For examples of these landholding patterns, see HCD 83:375, 86:283, 100:1, 102:105, 106:315, 107:536, 112:423, 113:455, 125:177 and 214:452. At the time of his death in 1863, Mark Joy owned two large wood lots and major shares in three schooners (Hancock County Probate Registry Docket 3728).

36. For records of the diphtheria plague, see Pendleton's journal entries from October 1862 through 1864.

Chapter 7

37. See the following entries in Dr. Pendleton's journal: June 7, 1852; July 22 and September 26, 1855; November 8, 1858; May 7, 1859; November 7, 1860; March–April 1860; November 1861; and December 1862. Ship and crew records can be found in Hahn, *History of Winter Harbor*. For land record transactions, see HCD 76:477; 81:133; 82:516, 520; 83:375;

86:283; 99:337; 102:104–05; 104:518; 106:181; 107:536; 112:423; 113:455; 126:164; 127:347; 136:288; 148:521; 206:467; 227:518; 315:188; and 341:422.

38. Crane, "If It's Ghosts You Want…" and testimony of Mr. Roy Bickford, Winter Harbor, July 2009.

39. See *Historical Researches*, 97, and testimony of Casper Sargent of Winter Harbor, August 2007.

Chapter 8

40. The decline of offshore banks fisheries is described in O'Leary, *Maine Sea Fisheries*, 360. See also Richard W. Judd, Edwin A. Churchill and Joel W. Eastman, eds., "Crisis and Decline in the Deep-Sea Fishing Industry" in *Maine: The Pine Tree State from Prehistory to the Present* (Orono: University of Maine Press, 1995), 391–400.

41. Joy's death is mentioned in Hancock County Probate Docket 2728. Information on plague losses and family removals can be found in Pendleton's journals for the years 1862–65. For land sales and transactions, see HCD 107:536, 116:8, 136:288, 150:447, 155:79, 160:480, 169:500, 175:426, 181:505, 214:452, 223:452, 235:55, 260:368 and 299:193. For information on fishing camp use at Pond Island and Little Moose at Arey's Cove, see Smallidge, *Musquito Harbor*, 238–39. Bickford's "devil cat" story is told by Jonas Crane in a Bangor news clipping (in Winter Harbor Historical Society) and also in Myra S. Earle, *Fond Memory: A Maine Coast Reminiscence* (Brunswick, ME: Biddle Publishing Co., 1993), 201.

42. Conditions for the rising lobster and weir fishery are summarized in Nathan Lipfert, "The Shore Fisheries, 1865–1930," in *Maine: The Pine Tree State*, 423–26. For information on local lobster storage enclosures, see Smallidge, *Musquito Harbor*, 237 and 241, and oral account from Casper Sargent. For information on Bunkers Harbor pounds built by Ezra Over and Frank Huckins, see *Historical Researches*, 97.

43. For Schoodic as "unused," see *Historical Researches*, 92. For sheepherding, see Day, *History of Maine Agriculture*, 188. Muir is quoted in Roderick Nash, *Wilderness and the American Mind* (New Haven, CT: Yale University Press, 1975), 127–30.

Chapter 9

44. American attitudes toward wilderness are classically chronicled in Nash's *Wilderness and the American Mind*, and attitudes toward nature and tourism are analyzed in Dona Brown, *Inventing New England: Regional Tourism in the Nineteenth Century* (Washington, D.C.: Smithsonian Books, 1997). The growth of the Bar Harbor resort market as of 1890 is described with insight by Samuel Adams Drake in "In and Out of Bar Harbor," *The Pine Tree Coast*, (Boston: Estes & Lauriat, 1891), 304–19.

45. For the arrival of rusticators in Winter Harbor, see Earle, *Fond Memory*, 280, and Smallidge, *Musquito Harbor*, 47–60. Hutchings's role in the new company is noted in *Bar Harbor Record*, February 8, 1899, 5. For land sales and transactions, see HCD 213:249, 218:157, 233:368, 236:350, 281:300, 286:1, 287:232 and 314:7.

46. The Gouldsboro Land Improvement Company prospectus was privately published in New York in 1889–90; key passages can be found on pp. 13–15. For information on other land developments, see *Maine Coast Cottager*, November 23 and December 7, 1895, and *Bar Harbor Record* 10, no. 54 (November 4, 1896): 4. E.J. Hammond's 1889 "The Winter Harbor Land Company" project is shown on a public-offering printed map located in the Gouldsboro Historical Society.

47. For information on Moore's career, see Smallidge, *Musquito Harbor*, 87–100; *Bar Harbor Record* 10, nos. 34–42 (August–September 1896); and *Bar Harbor Record*, May 10, 1889, 1. The Winter Harbor Town Office map from this era may reflect landholdings of about 1896–97. In *Bar Harbor Record* 12, no. 50 (November 9, 1898): 1, Moore reported negotiating his purchases over three years, or since about 1895. Moore's railroad efforts are noted in *Bar Harbor Record* 11, no. 46 (September 18, 1897): 5, and his roadwork is described in *Bar Harbor Record* 11, no. 52 (October 27, 1897): 3, and Smallidge, *Musquito Harbor*, 98–99. See also *Bar Harbor Record* 11, no. 55 (November 17, 1897): 4; *Bar Harbor Record* 12, no. 2 (February 9, 1898): 5; *Bar Harbor Record* 12, no. 50 (November 9, 1898): 1; *Bar Harbor Record* 11, no. 52 (October 27, 1897): 2; and Moore's eulogy in *Bar Harbor Record*, July 5, 1899, 1. For land transactions, see HCD 318:171 and 334:448.

Chapter 10

48. For Moore's heirs' transactions, see HCD 341:177, 376:256 and 534:209–11. Winter Harbor town tax assessments for 1908, 1925, 1926 and 1927 are located in the town office, Winter Harbor, Maine.

49. Information on land use in this period comes from an October 2007 conversation with Casper Sargent and Smallidge, *Musquito Harbor*, 238, as well as the testimony of Allan Smallidge and Katherine Delaney Ross. Bickford family records can be found in Johnson, *Early Families*, 31. School requests and Lower Harbor pound description can be found in Smallidge, *Musquito Harbor*, 158.

50. For origins of Acadia National Park and Schoodic, see George Dorr, *The Story of Acadia National Park*, Book 2 (Bar Harbor, ME: Acadia Publishing Co., 1985), 25–38. Also, ANP cultural resource manager Lee Terzis, talk at Schoodic, May 2005. For information on deeds of gift to Hancock Trustees and Acadia National Park, see HCD 607:361–62, 623:381 and 640:333.

51. Tax pressures on Acadia wild land due to the influence of real estate and timber interests are reported in Ann Roberts Rockefeller, *Mr. Rockefeller's Roads* (Rockport, ME: Down East Books, 1990), 44. Roberts contrasts Rockefeller and Dorr's views on land use in *Mr. Rockefeller's Roads*, 63–68. See also Smallidge, *Musquito Harbor*, 101. Early park conditions were described by Winter Harbor resident Casper Sargent.

Chapter 11

52. For park development at Schoodic, see Dorr, *Story of Acadia National Park*, 35–38, and Smallidge, *Musquito Harbor*, 101–02. Also, National Park Service, "A Cultural Landscape Inventory: Schoodic Peninsula" (2001) cites a May 22, 1930 memo from Rockefeller Jr. regarding his site visit to Big Moose Island.

53. For a chronology of park acquisition and construction, see National Park Service, "Cultural Landscape Inventory," 9–13. See also James Moreira et al, "The Civilian Conservation Corps at Acadia National Park" (2009), 171. Information also gleaned from oral testimony of Casper Sargent, 2008, and Acadia National Park Archives records and photos. For land transactions, see HCD 607:361–62 and 645:513.

54. Charles Eliot's views on "the public" taken from a letter to fellow trustee L.M. Luquer, August 23, 1903, quoted in William Horner, MD, "Deasy: A Maine Man," *Chebacco* (Mount Desert Island Historical Society) 11 (2010): 17. Views on wilderness gleaned from Nash, *Wilderness and the American Mind*, 122, 149–50, and John Muir, "The American Forests," *Atlantic Monthly* 80 (1897): 146.

Chapter 12

55. Base description taken from Smallidge, *Musquito Harbor*, 101–02, and conversation with Dale Woodward, Gouldsboro Historical Society, October 5, 2009. Information on Navy operations "Classic Bullseye" and "Classic Wizard" gleaned from testimony of David Phaneuf and Larry Peterson (March 2013) and Haven Ross (July 2012). Information on road closure obtained per conversation with Allan Smallidge, August 2005.
56. See "Cultural Landscape Inventory," 9–13.
57. See HCD 517:139.
58. For more on the Marin drawing, see John Wilmerding, *The Artist's Mount Desert: American Painters on the Maine Coast* (Princeton, NJ: Princeton University Press, 1994), 125. Hartley's work habits were described in conversation with Miriam Colwell, September 2007. Amy Clampitt's "Low Tide at Schoodic" published in *The New Yorker* 60, no. 18 (August 6, 1984): 30.

Chapter 13

59. For information on the evolution of Schoodic Woods, see Woodlot Alternatives Inc., "An Ecological Assessment of the 1,600-Acre Parcel at Schoodic Peninsula," September 1996, located in Acadia National Park Archives. For land sales, see HCD 218:157, 233:368 and 376:256.
60. See Jacqueline Weaver, "Concept for Schoodic Eco-Resort," *Ellsworth American*, May 22, 2008, and "Conservancy: Eco-Resort Threat to Schoodic," *Ellsworth American*, July 31, 2008.
61. Jacqueline Weaver, "Campground Is Planned for Schoodic," *Ellsworth American*, February 21, 2013. See also Earl Brechlin, "Schoodic Land Sale Means No Eco-resort," *Ellsworth American*, December 22, 2011.

INDEX

ABOUT THE AUTHOR

Allen Workman has lived in the shadow of beautiful Schoodic Point since age fourteen. In his later teens, he worked in Maine as lobsterman's sternman and in shipbuilding before pursuing a forty-year career as an editor in educational publishing. He retired to become a Maine curmudgeon and local historian in the Schoodic Peninsula region, giving occasional talks on the changing landscape of this most enchanting section of Acadia National Park.

Visit us at
www.historypress.net
....
This title is also available as an e-book

www.ingramcontent.com/pod-product-compliance
Lightning Source LLC
Chambersburg PA
CBHW060804100426
42813CB00004B/941